APPALACHIAN HERITAGE

VOL. 47, NO. 1
WINTER 2019

ESTABLISHED IN 1973

PUBLISHED QUARTERLY
by Berea College
CPO 2166
205 N. Main Street
Berea, KY, 40404

www.appalachianheritage.net

 Periodicals postage paid at Berea, Kentucky, and at additional mailing offices. ISSN# 03632318.

Electronic submissions only at www.appalachianheritage.net

Distributed by the University of North Carolina Press. Basic subscription price: $30/year for individuals, $40/year for institutions. For subscription requests and inquiries, visit the magazine's website, email uncpress_journals@unc.edu, or call 919.962.4201.

CONTENTS

INTERVIEW

CRAFT ESSAY

BOOK REVIEWS

EDITOR'S NOTE

JASON HOWARD

At a recent conference focused on Appalachia, a prospective contributor approached our magazine's exhibit booth and began perusing a recent issue. She had submitted some work during our last reading period, she told a student worker, and she indicated her familiarity with some of our contributors. Then she proceeded to make a stunning declaration. She and her work were more Appalachian than anyone or anything we have published. And further, she was more Appalachian than anyone at the conference.

Upon receiving word of this encounter, I moved through several stages of processing. My hackles rose in defense of my student and authors. Then I shook my head at the sheer lack of logic displayed by the prospective contributor—it is never a good strategy to demean a publication in which one wants their work to appear, let alone to imply one's work is superior to that of others. Finally, I was left with the bedrock of her claims about the magazine and the conference. What, exactly, did she mean about being more Appalachian?

Did she trek miles through the mountains each spring looking for poke? Was she talking about her recipe for cornbread? (*Never any sugar*, I imagined her sneering.) Did she shun any music that did not include some variation of guitar, banjo, mandolin, autoharp and fiddle? Would the addition of a piano—or, whisper it, an electric guitar—dilute the supposed authenticity of the music? How could someone scan a room of scholars and writers, many of whom have devoted decades of study and craft in relation to a place, and imply that her work counted more than theirs?

We all have notions of what it means to be from Appalachia or to be Appalachian, and those can be entertaining and enlightening to discuss. But purity tests are a different thing entirely, and to me they wreak of cultural eugenics.

Does one have to be born in Appalachia and, if so, where is that exactly? Are we to accept the expansive political map of the Appalachian Regional Commission? Or are we to restrict citizenship, as many do, to central Appalachia—eastern Kentucky, West Virginia, southwest Virginia, east Tennessee and western North Carolina? (If the latter, this precludes James Still, widely celebrated as one of the most significant Appalachian writers; Annie Dillard, winner of the Pulitzer Prize for *Pilgrim at Tinker Creek*, a book set in southwest Virginia; and bell hooks, the internationally renowned feminist, critic, and creative writer who has long lived in, studied, and written about the region.)

Does one have to solely set their writing in Appalachia? (Such a test would mean the likes of Barbara Kingsolver, Mary Lee Settle, Silas House, Denise Giardina, Wilma Dykeman, and numerous others sadly do not qualify.)

Does one have to always live in Appalachia to count? (Farewell to Lee Smith, Harriette Simpson Arnow, Nikki Giovanni, Lisa Alther, Henry Louis Gates, Ann Pancake, Jayne Anne Phillips, Dorothy Allison, Gurney Norman, Crystal Wilkinson, George Ella Lyon, Wiley Cash, Maurice Manning, and many others.)

With such restrictive criteria Appalachian literature would be left with a pretty spare canon, which is but one reason that, as editor of this publication, I have rejected the notion of purity tests—an ethos that provides the underpinning of our mission statement. We are a literary magazine that "showcases the work of emerging and established writers through Appalachia and beyond, offering readers literature that is thoughtful, innovative, and revelatory."

Just because "Appalachian" appears in our name does not mean we are a publication subsumed by the past. There is history to such an assumption: it is a pernicious stereotype that first emerged when the very idea of Appalachia as a distinct region was constructed 150 years ago by local color writers and others. Since then the region has often been defined as the American counterpoint—a place with its eyes on the past instead of the future. A region isolated from the outside world, where time has stood still. A simpler place, quainter, more bucolic—or alternatively, more primitive and violent—than the rest of the country.

But, of course, this is not true. Appalachia is, and has always been, a microcosm of America—a place directly connected to the triumphs, tribulations, and issues of the rest of the country.

While we certainly honor the past, our orientation is on writing from contemporary Appalachia that strives to encompass the diverse identities and issues of its people. We seek to offer a complex view of a complex region that goes beyond saintly grannies and mossy fenceposts.

Further, we believe the very notion of Appalachia is not firm but porous. In our pages, we often feature work set in the region. But we also pay tribute to the experience of the Appalachian diaspora—the people who have moved beyond the region's geographic borders but who are still spiritually Appalachian, even when they are sometimes several generations removed. We explore urban Appalachia, which has historically been underrepresented. And we even occasionally offer work from other mountain or rural cultures as points of comparison and reflection.

In short, our notions of Appalachia, its people, and its literature are complex and nuanced. This region is expansive—it cannot be contained by one county, one race, one ethnicity, one gender, one class, one sexual orientation, one gender identity, one religion, one accent, one dialect, one era, or one age group. There are many Appalachias and many Appalachian experiences, and as long as I am editor of this publication, we will seek to showcase them in all their vibrant, complicated glory. ■

2018 DENNY C. PLATTNER AWARDS

The annual Plattner Awards were established in 1995 by Kenneth and Elissa Plattner to honor their late son and his love of writing. The awards are given to the finest pieces of fiction, creative nonfiction, and poetry that appeared in *Appalachian Heritage* during the previous year. Winners receive a $200 prize, and both winners and honorable mentions are awarded a handsome cherry wooden book rack designed and manufactured by Berea College Crafts.

FICTION

Judged by Elaine Fowler Palencia, author of Brier Country *and* Small Caucasian Woman

Winner: Shaun Turner, "Funeral March"
Honorable Mention: Chris Holbrook, "Surface Level"

CREATIVE NONFICTION

Judged by Beth Newberry, award-winning essayist and editor

Winner: Monic Ductan, "Fantasy Worlds"
Honorable Mention: Jake Maynard, "Barely Runnable"

POETRY

Judged by L.S. McKee, award-winning poet and teacher

Winner: Lyrae Van Clief-Stefanon, "Scorned, He Implodes, 1999, from the Series *Soul Erased* by Joyce Scott"
Honorable Mention: Savannah Sipple, "What We Tell Ourselves"

EARTH, SKY, TREES

DAVIS ENLOE

The doctor's office turned absurd, disconnected from Black Mountain Cancer Center. When the floor began to gyrate, Joe wanted to run across the tilting room, ram his head through the large glass window and scream, "Who put those damn mountains there? Why is that stupid moon out in the middle of the day?" He wanted to shake the doctor until he agreed what he'd said was preposterous, an offense to the Almighty that cannot stand.

"As quickly as this has spread—is spreading," the doctor's flat voice continued. "Frankly, with it already past your lymph nodes—"

"Plain language," Libby said, his wife speaking plainly herself.

"It's in your liver and pancreas. Stage IV. Mortality rate is high."

"How high?" Libby said.

Joe gripped the sides of the chair that threatened to tip over, though a part of him wanted to fall, to kick on the floor like an out of control two-year old. He struggled to regain his balance, to shut everything out. Still, there was that doctor's dull voice telling him his life was never going to be the same.

"Ten percent chance of survival," the doctor said. Then, looking away, "Maybe."

More aggressive the treatment, better the chances, the doctor droned on. Critical to start treatment immediately. Expensive, yes, but there were ways to reduce costs.

Joe wanted to demand that he and Libby trade places—that he give her his organs. He wanted to let go of the chair, grab that doctor by his clean white coat and shout in his face until the room stopped spinning, until things were right again, until the foolish man said Libby was not sick, was not going to die. Instead, Joe sat there. Stunned. Silent.

"Let's go," Libby said. "Not wasting my last breaths in a hospital." Like a mother holding a bewildered child's hand, Libby led Joe down the fun-house stairs and into the twisted sunlight.

■ ■ ■

Over the next six months, Joe tended to his wife's daily needs, bathed her, washed her soiled clothes, and arranged friends or relatives to sit with her while he cut wood. Her brown hair had turned grey and the severe weight loss had left her frail. After months of decline and unrelenting pain, Libby stopped talking about cosmic identity, her love of stars, or visiting New Mexico.

"I want you to do it," Lib finally said.

He'd heard her wrong, Joe thought. No way she'd asked him to kill her. He shook out his *Citizen-Times* and went back to reading.

"I'd do it for you," she said.

Joe folded his paper. Leah, the Hospice nurse in the kitchen washing dishes, hummed a church hymn. He couldn't remember the name of the song, but his mother had always called it "Jesus is Calling." He poked in the fire and orange embers scattered like runaway planets from a faraway galaxy. Then the embers were gone, the galaxy wiped out in seconds.

"You going to pretend you didn't hear me?"

Leah, shaking water from her hands, poked her head into the room long enough to say that if they didn't need anything else she was leaving. Before Joe had a chance to thank her and see her out she was gone.

Joe leaned the poker against the fireplace. "Was hoping I'd heard you wrong. Don't ask me to murder you."

The walls seemed closer, the ceiling lower than only seconds before. Joe wanted to leave, to escape hearing whatever was coming next.

"I am asking. The man I love should stop this pain—the man who loves me."

Joe sat on the floor beside his wife's bed. It was mercy, she told him, not murder. Think of it as opening a prison cell, setting the prisoner free.

"You're asking me to commit the worst kind of wrong."

But was she? If things were reversed, would he not want her to end his suffering? He loved her beyond any measure, so how was it wrong to end her pain? She was only going to get worse.

"Jesus, Joe," she said, "they do it for sick dogs. Do I not deserve the same mercy given a dog?"

"They give a dog a shot," Joe said, holding back his anger. "I don't have that shot!" He imagined her trying to breathe—an animal in a gas chamber gasping for breath. "And if I did have it, I wouldn't use it." But maybe it was a simple act of compassion. No light was flashing on in the head of brilliant scientist, a miracle cure compounded into a colorful pill. Libby was going to die, and soon. What right did anyone have to insist she suffer to her last breath? "If?" Joe said,

He saw himself pressing a pillow over Libby's face, but as soon as she struggled he stopped and slung the pillow across the room.

"How? Smother you? Pounce on you in the dark?" He saw himself pressing a pillow over Libby's face, but as soon as she struggled he stopped and slung the pillow across the room. He wanted to apologize for the thought, yet he was furious at Libby for causing him to think it. "How about a knock on the head with a 4-lb sledge?" he said. "That should do it."

"Don't be an asshole, Joe. Leave the pain pills by the bed. For God's sake, think about it."

Joe hurried out of the room, unsure if he was angry at Lib's request or because he lacked the courage to honor it. Was he nothing more than a common coward? As he turned out the bedroom lights, Libby called after him. "There's something else I need—after I'm gone."

"What?" Joe said.

"Promise me."

Hell, no. He wasn't promising a damn thing. "Not in the mood," he said, "for promises."

"Cut the bull. If you're too chicken-shit to end this pain, at least do one thing for me after I'm gone."

By the time Joe pulled a chair up to her bedside, his anger, like the embers, had burned away. God, he loved her. He wanted to touch her, to crawl in the bed beside her, to hold her. He wanted her to never die.

"I promise, but I better not regret it."

What was life going to be like without her? Would he sit alone by the fire, Joe wondered, hear her voice in another room and hurry to find her? Would he burst into tears when someone asked him how he was doing?

"I'm going to leave you a list," Libby said. You have to do everything on the list exactly the way it's written."

■ ■ ■

A few weeks later, Joe stood at the back of the ambulance urging the EMS techs to double-check the straps. "Don't worry, Lib," he said, "I'll be there when these doors open."

Seconds after the transport turned right onto Highway 221 toward Ellenton, Libby died. He could not have explained it, but Joe experienced the moment it happened. Not because Joe was a spiritual creature. He wasn't. He didn't deny the possibility of a God, it just didn't scare him to believe there wasn't one. But God, or no God, with Libby's last breath, Joe felt a stab of pain, like his spine had been stripped from his body. He pulled over and rested his head on the steering wheel. It hurt to know she'd been alone—beyond his ability to help, beyond the reach of hope or love. Maybe, Joe reasoned, her last joy was watching the Blue Ridge Mountains fade outside the ambulance's square rear windows. Who was he fooling—more likely she was thinking about the damned promise.

■ ■ ■

Two hours after the ambulance had pulled away from his house, Joe stood in front of Mr. Atkins, the hospital administrator sitting in a creaky wooden chair behind a huge desk. He was sorry, but county regulations prevented the release of Libby's body back to Joe.

"I promised," Joe said, "to cremate her body in a private ceremony—like she wanted."

"You're not licensed," Mr. Atkins said. "Don't have the proper cremation oven. Sheriff Harvey would charge you with desecration, say I was complicit."

"I got plenty of white oak. And I intend to keep my vow." Joe stood hands-on-hips, leaning over at the waist. "Besides, Harve is Libby's favorite uncle. Don't make me call him."

But the little man with round glasses didn't flinch. "Your promise means nothing to me," he said. "You're not about to call the law on yourself."

Of course, he wasn't going to call the law. Silly thing to say, but something had to give for the plan to move forward.

"You release Libby's body right damn now."

As if Mr. Atkins might wilt, Joe waited. Tomorrow he would get Libby's body from Conley Funeral Home.

"And if you're thinking about asking Jim Conley," Mr. Atkins said, "his hands are tied with the same rope as mine."

Damn if he would wait on Atkins to give in. And damn if he would wait another day. Joe shook Mr. Atkins' hand and thanked him. Eight hours later, just before midnight, he pulled his pickup into the morgue's rear parking lot.

■ ■ ■

Beyond his headlights, the grey building reminded Joe of a battleship with a large white door on one side. He sat worrying through his plan. What had he forgotten? Where was the weak link? He thought about Lib, how it seemed only yesterday they'd been sitting at their breakfast table with Joe furious at Eddie Drake, the furniture plant manager where Libby worked. The ventilation was bad and Drake had been ignoring the safety warnings, choosing to pay low government fines rather than spend money on upgrades. For months, Libby had worked in a cloud of yellow glue haze. Sometimes, even her breath had smelled like glue.

"After the holidays," Libby'd said, "I'll quit. Right after the bonus. With the extra money we can camp longer in the Chihuahuan. See more constellations, and still take time to look at property for retirement."

"Jesus, Lib," Joe'd said, "it's only July." He'd counted on his fingers as he called the months out by name. "That's six more months of breathing that crap. What good are retirement plans if your health is ruined?"

Joe shook the truck's steering wheel. "I should have stopped it," he said. To focus on the task ahead, he closed his eyes. For sure, the weakest link was Wink Watts, janitor and night-watchman at the hospital. What if he'd balked, gone back on his promise to help steal Libby's body? Maybe Harve was waiting inside to slap on handcuffs. Harve was tricky to read. Sometimes he was chummy, sometimes standoffish, like he was still mad about Joe, twenty years ago and two years out of high school, getting off scot-free on marijuana possession. But that was when Harve had just gotten out of the Army, was Mr. Spit-and-Polish, and had gone to work for the county as a by-the-book deputy.

Joe switched on the overhead light and from the center console pulled out a fifth of Crown Royal and a bank envelope stuffed with money. He counted out five twenties and dropped the rest back in the console. Next, he pulled out the small yellow notepad Libby had used to make her list. At the top of the first page, written in her shaky blue scrawl: Joe's List. Beneath that, *Step One: Prepare the workshop for Libby's return.* Joe had scribbled in tasks of his own to complete before bringing his wife's body back from the hospital: *plow a firebreak around the tobacco barn, gather pine and oak, find (or buy) a lighter, gather old rags, fill both gas cans.* After rubbing his chin for a bit, he took the rest of the money.

He flipped the pages, tapping a finger at a note here and there, then cut the engine. When he lowered the window, cooler night air rushed into the cab. From the rear of his pickup, Joe

He flipped the pages, tapping a finger at a note here and there, then cut the engine. When he lowered the window, cooler night air rushed into the cab.

scanned the emergency room parking lot a couple hundred yards away. Thank goodness, Ellenton General was no high-tech security facility. Down the long grassy hill from the hospital, across the creek, a police car passed beneath streetlights. It slowed, then went on. Joe ducked beside his truck. That's all he needed, a deputy sheriff, or worse, Harve himself pulling up on him. None of Harve's business. No one's business, but his own—and Libby's. But what if Wink hadn't shut off the alarm?

On the rear seat were several couch cushions and a blue quilt with a white-star pattern—items she'd written under *Step Two: Prepare the truck to receive Libby's vessel.* After he positioned the cushions along the front edge of the seat, he shook out the quilt and held it to his face. It smelled of cedar and mothballs. It was obvious which patches he'd stitched, the sloppy ones. But it was theirs, by God, not another one like it on the face of this or any other earth. If he'd only stood his ground, refused to let her work at that damn furniture plant. If he'd burned it to its foundation. "If," he said.

Joe stretched the quilt across the seat, letting half fall over the cushions and onto the floorboard. He smoothed the quilt, tugging its edges, then caught the moonlight on his watch. Almost time. He checked off Step Two then flipped a page, *Step Three: Bring Libby's vessel home from the hospital.* He jabbed the notepad with his stubby pencil. "Always scheming," he whispered. "Weren't you, Lib?"

Part of what he had loved most about Libby—no, not *had* loved. What he loved in this moment, was the conviction with which she believed in an afterlife. She'd believed that at her death she would return to the universe, fold back into its eternal energy, live forever as part of something larger than herself. She'd described herself as a universal creature from the cosmic womb, one destined to return to the cosmos to emerge again as who knows what, or when. Joe thought otherwise: You die, you're done. Like a light switch—one second, you're on, the next you may as well have never lived. He believed in what he could see and talk to. Nothing else.

And what the hell had Libby ever seen in him, Joe wondered. He'd never had the nerve to ask, but now he wished he had. He knew damn well what had drawn him to her, that when she touched his forearm he felt cherished, but more importantly, special. He mattered. With Libby, he'd always known things would be okay. But now they weren't.

As he approached the morgue entrance, the floodlights clicked on. Joe leapt sideways, landing flat beneath a hedge.

Sorry shit, Wink. Had to forget something, didn't he? The damp leaves smelled like wet goat. Joe shaded his eyes. A few seconds later, he brushed himself off and placed his ear against the cool metal door. He waited, then rapped lightly three times, two seconds between each knock. He had cocked a fist to bang on the door when a voice inside asked who the hell was it.

"Huckleberry Hound?" Joe said. "Kill that light."

The outside floods went dark.

"We got to par-lay," Wink said through the door.

Joe kicked the door and threatened to crack open Wink's head, scatter his marbles all over the hospital floor, but Wink held his ground, said Joe wasn't going to do shit on the wrong side of the door, that a fifth of Crown wasn't enough and if he didn't have 200 scratch the deal was nixed.

Joe counted out ten 20's, then kicked the door again, but harder. The deadbolt clicked, light spilled out.

"Try anything," Wink said, "law'll be on you like Satan on a Lutheran."

Joe punched Wink in the solar plexus and shoved him backwards.

"You was always," Wink said, gasping, "a mean bastard."

The room smelled like formaldehyde, bleach, and a hint of lemon. White four-inch tiles with black grout covered the floor and all the walls. A wide stainless-steel sink took up one wall and scattered around the room was equipment that looked like it belonged in a science lab. Opposite the sink were eight stainless steel doors—two rows of four.

"A mean bastard, huh?" Joe said. "So, no surprise when I strap your ass to that table." Joe pointed to the middle of the room at a porcelain autopsy table supported on one end by a large pedestal. The table had an inlaid stainless panel that looked like a fish skeleton. "Maybe I'll cut you open like a trout, wash you off with that sprayer hose." Joe grabbed Wink by the shirt and stuffed the loose bills into his pocket. "Take the liquor, get the hell out."

Wink snatched the fifth of Crown Royal. "All that," he said, "for a swallow of swill." He hurried toward the double doors leading into the hospital, calling back, "You still here in ten minutes, I'm calling Harve. Say I caught you B&E."

"Because that's the kind of shit you are," Joe said.

"Only reason I'm helping, Lib was kin." Then, before disappearing, "Maybe I'll call the law for giggles. That's the kind of *shit* I am."

Joe rolled the gurney over to Libby's vault. He ran a finger around the brass frame holding his wife's name card: *L. Raines*. Like a boat lifting over an ocean swell, emotions heaved inside. He tugged, taking his time swinging the door open. When the shelf rolled quicker than Joe expected, he slowed it with both hands. At least they'd had the decency to cover her. But he refused to look at Libby, at her body. It wasn't her. Libby had lived in spectacular color, he thought. He imagined her body as spent cardboard tubing from a Roman candle. Still, it wasn't that simple, because it *was* Libby's body. Focus, he told himself. Step-by-step, as promised. Joe lifted his wife's body onto the gurney.

In the months before Libby died, Joe had been unable to hold and comfort her. Just stroking her hair had caused Libby discomfort. Because the movement of the mattress had shot pain through her body, he'd been unable to sit on the edge of the bed. That'd been the hardest part—denied the chance to comfort her. Yet, it was a curious thing, the not touching, how not touching had drawn him closer, caused him to love her more.

Outside the morgue, Joe lifted Libby's body and kicked the gurney over beneath the hedge. As he carried her to the truck, he whispered, "So light."

Joe slid her body onto the back seat. "Comfortable, baby?" he said. He snugged cushions against her, then lifted the quilt from the floorboard and draped it across her. "I'm not going to kill Drake," he said. "But I might burn his damn plant down—make it Step Eight."

■ ■ ■

Step Four: Carry Libby's vessel to Darlington and behold the stars. (Don't take my body out of the truck—that would be weird). Joe sat a while. Where would he go after this? Not where would he live, but where would he find peace? Libby had been the only woman he'd not eventually disappointed. The only woman to fill him with not only joy, but contentment. He remembered the January morning his mother had died, kicked by a skittish Holstein. The ice crystals had crunched into the hard clay as he'd raced through the cold air. "Stop your whimpering," his father had told him at her funeral. "Everybody dies. Ain't nobody special."

Joe took the back way, familiar dirt roads that cut across land where he cut pulp wood. Dogs barked deep in the woods. He expected Wink to call the law—make it look like he was innocent. This route was longer than the eight miles by hardtop but provided better cover. At Darlington Creek, he eased over the large round rocks and into the water, stopping midway across. He glanced at the dash clock: 1:45. To make sure he'd not been followed, Joe glanced into the rearview mirror. He half expected to see Harve sitting in his squad car—not that this was any of his damn business. Instead, there was Libby, sitting up, smiling like she'd just played the world's greatest practical joke. Joe jumped, but then caught himself. He was no fool. It was night, bad light. He'd been under a lot of stress. He closed his eyes. "A figment, that's all," he said. "A mental made-up-something-another." When he opened his eyes, the apparition was gone. No smiling Libby. No scowling Harve. Other than tree frogs, crickets, and the sound of the rushing creek, he was alone. He resisted the urge to reach between the seats and take Libby's pulse.

At the front of the truck he leaned against the grill. Cool water reached his knees. "Think that's pretty funny, scaring me? Maybe I should just float you down the creek like baby Moses' twin sister."

On some nights, when the stars had seemed brightest, they'd stayed for hours at Darlington Creek—sometimes until the sun brightened the horizon. It was close to home, but far enough from town to escape artificial light and other people. The stars were lovely, but to Joe most of it looked the same. Water pressed and gurgled against his legs. Moonlight reflecting off the silvery clouds reminded Joe of the Milky Way.

"Look, Lib," Joe said, "Orion is out strong tonight." Then he chuckled, as if Libby was listening and knew he didn't have a clue where to find Orion. "What?" he said. "I thought this was the time of year you could see the bastard." Joe used the front bumper to slide up onto the truck's hood. "But what if I don't want to leave Ellenton?" he said. "I know I promised, and I will go to New Mexico, I think. What if I don't want to sell the house? What if afterwards, after I've seen the stars from the desert, I want to come home, be close to our memories?" Joe glanced back toward Libby's body.

With the completion of the fourth task, Joe waded back. "It's not like you're ever going to know," he said, climbing in, "whether or not I go out west."

Ten minutes later he'd parked behind the barn and was carrying Libby into her workshop, an old tobacco barn with hundred-year-old logs that were each over a foot square. He'd fixed it up for her to use as private space for reflection, a place to tinker with old clocks. An unusual hobby for a woman, he'd thought, but time had always interested her—"how humans cling to it," she'd said. "As if time is more than an imagined concept by which we manage our lives." He placed Libby's body on the large work table.

What would he do with all her tools—the micro-screwdrivers, tweezers, files, the assortment of peculiar precision instruments that felt alien to Joe, so different from his ax and chainsaw, but natural extensions of Libby. He considered sweeping it all into a duffle bag, but it seemed right to leave her things in place. That's what the Egyptians would have done—buried their pharaohs with their possessions. Maybe Lib would need them in her next life.

"You sure," he said, "this is what you want?"

Libby had explained that she could not join the universal dimension until her body had been properly attended...

Of course, she was sure. What use was there in asking a dead person a question—certainly not a rhetorical one. Libby had explained that she could not join the universal dimension until her body had been properly attended—that she would remain tethered to earth until Joe released her. He'd tried to believe in Libby's idea of the hereafter, but Joe had always been grounded in the things around him—earth, sky, trees. Still, it pained him to realize that once they were both gone, their memories might start to fade—as if neither had ever lived, had never loved the other.

Joe sat on a stool beside Libby's body, as if waiting for her to reassure him it was okay to proceed. He thought of the conversation they'd had a few weeks before she died.

"Why can't memories be like diamonds," he'd said. "Be beautiful and last forever?"

"Aren't diamonds beautiful," Libby'd said, "because of how they refract light?"

"Oh God," Joe'd said, "another school lesson."

"The diamond is the medium for the beauty we see when we hold it in the light," she'd continued. "We need the diamond to experience the beauty of refracted light, but the diamond itself is not the—."

"I get it," Joe'd said testily. "The spark matters, not the sparkplug."

He slid the sheet off Libby's body. Under the white light angling through a skylight she looked twenty years older than her forty-eight-year-old body. Her joints were swollen and twisted; her hands and toes gnarled. Her hair was white. It was then he saw the flaw in Libby's explanation, because for him both the diamond and the refracted light were gone. Nothing made sense. It all seemed like madness, an unwinnable contest: love, life, loss. For the second time, a swell of emotion rose inside of Joe. He closed his eyes, then he kissed her hands, her face, her lips.

"So sorry, baby," he said.

From near her feet, Joe picked up a folded bedsheet—light blue with faint yellow seashells. Shaking it in the air, he let the sheet settle across her body, then tucked it loosely around. *Step Five: Place Libby's vessel in her workshop and drape it with her favorite sheet—you know the one.*

After opening the windows, Joe carried in several armloads of oak firewood from the woodshed. "No, don't get up," he said. "I got this."

To complete the pyre that he'd left unfinished—allowing room to place Libby's body—he stacked wood in front of the worktable. Next, he brought in two cans of gas that he poured on the floor. He soaked old rags and stuffed them between the sticks of wood. After splashing gas on the inside walls, he walked around the barn, sloshing fuel on the hundred-year-old timbers.

"I don't feel good about this, Lib," he said.

He pulled a handkerchief from his pocket and lit it with a Bic lighter. *Step Six: Douse Libby's studio with gasoline and set it afire.* Now, only one step left, *Step Seven: Stay with Libby until the fire has consumed her form, then release her with the rising smoke.* But instead of lighting the pyre, Joe dropped the burning handkerchief to the ground and stepped on the flame. Not so fast, he thought. What's the damn hurry? I've got to think this through. When she was gone—when her body was gone—that would be it. The chance to do the right thing would be gone forever. Libby would be gone forever. "Can't do this, Lib. This time, not getting your way."

■ ■ ■

Sixteen years earlier, when he and Libby had first met, Joe'd thought it an accident. Years later, he'd learned Libby's sense of direction that day had not been as bad as she'd claimed.

Joe smiled to remember how she'd waited months for him to pay attention to her at the flea market, at community Bingo. Getting him to talk, she'd said, was like trying to kick start an old Harley-Davidson—he would spit out a few words then sputter to a stop.

On a warm September morning, he'd been cutting a load of firewood, and Libby had known exactly where he was—two miles into the woods and several hundred yards off an old logging road that cut through the forest. The trees were in a low area with soggy ground. Mosquitoes were swarming, yellow jackets zipping around, and it was too damn hot for September.

Long before he'd seen Libby's car, he heard the engine revving as the car bounced in and out of mud holes. When the Subaru stopped next to Joe, there'd been a large telescope strapped to the car's luggage rack. "Is this the way," Libby'd said, "to Table Mountain?"

At first, he'd thought someone was playing a joke on him. No one had ever got lost where he was cutting wood—certainly not a pretty woman with an electric smile.

"This is the way to nowhere," Joe'd said. "Except where you already are." He'd pointed in the opposite direction. "Table Mountain is six miles southeast."

Joe'd stood with both hands on the end of his axe handle. It'd made him nervous when Libby didn't respond, as if she was checking him for fleas.

"I've packed enough food for two," she'd said. "Fried chicken, potato salad, rhubarb pie."

Joe'd swatted away a yellow jacket. Then he'd looked at the wood left to cut. "Rhubarb pie?"

This was the first of many times Joe had unstrapped the scuffed telescope from the top of the Subaru. Though he couldn't say how many times he tied the telescope to a backpack and toted it to a remote mountain top, he was fond of saying he never again ate another peanut butter sandwich. It wasn't true, but he knew Libby loved hearing him say it. They would sit on granite overlooks and watch for a peculiar alignment of Jupiter and Venus. They'd watched Mars come close to earth, its polar ice caps visible through the telescope.

"Isn't this amazing?" Libby'd once said. "Loking into the universe that mothered us. Glimpsing a tiny part of our cosmic process?"

"Yes," Joe'd answered. "*Amazing*."

But what had interested Joe most was being on a mountain with Libby where he'd felt not just needed, but essential. He never questioned his inner life, life before earth, or life after. It was enough that he'd ended up on a granite cliff, loving Libby. There was genius in his simplicity, Libby had told him—to be unburdened by tomorrow, next week, or a next life.

■ ■ ■

After stomping out the burning handkerchief, Joe headed to the barn. A couple of minutes later, he returned carrying a sledgehammer and a Coleman lantern. With the stride of a determined man, he walked over to Libby's old Subaru parked beneath a massive red oak. He sat the lantern on top of a large humped root. He'd been after Libby for years to get rid of the old beater that sat broken more than it ran, but now Joe was glad to see it.

In one swift motion, Joe lifted and swung the big hammer down on the hood of the old Subaru, shattering the quiet and causing dogs to bark off in the distance. "You brought her into my life," he said. "You're the reason."

First the hood, then the headlights. Next the windshield, then the window glass. As Joe worked his way around the car, his shadow lurched like a primal spirit, one struggling to break loose from its earthly fetter. He took his time on the roof, circling the car again as he pounded. "You want me to burn your body, do you? Your vessel," he said, calling back to the barn. "Speak up, Lib. Just light you on fire and forget you. That what you had in mind? Strike a match, get over it."

It took him a while to beat down the car's roof and he started to tire. Finally, he sat down to rest. "Maybe I will, Lib," he said. "Maybe I'll forget I ever knew you." Then the shadow was back at it, jerking, swaying, crushing doors, beating at wheels, smashing any part of the car he'd not already whacked. The dogs started barking again.

"How about I burn your damn list, take you back to the morgue," he said, starting to cry. "What if I want to kick around in mud like an angry boar. Maybe I need to climb to the top of Mt. Mitchell and curse God. Maybe I need to do this my way." Like an angry Olympic hammer thrower, Joe spun twice and slung the sledgehammer. It made a woofing sound as it sailed end to end until it thudded against the tobacco barn and caromed into the dark. "I don't want to live in New Mexico without you," Joe said, sinking to his knees beside the car. "You even think about that?

■ ■ ■

When Sheriff Harvey pulled up thirty minutes later, his cruiser squeaking to a stop, Joe was sitting cross-legged on the battered car's hood.

"Joe?" the sheriff said, approaching from behind.

"Car needs springs," Joe said.

"Let it squeak—getting a new one soon," Harve said. "This used to be Lib's Subaru."

"Still is, "Joe said. "You going to arrest me?"

"Ought to," Harve said. "For beating that drug possession."

"You still pissed about that?"

"Just saying, Joe."

Leaning against the beat-down Subaru, the sheriff took a pack of cigarettes out of his pants. Early sunlight rimmed the hills and a morning breeze stirred. The sheriff took off his hat.

"I'm guessing Libby's in the tobacco barn."

Joe nodded. "I couldn't do it."

Harve nodded. "She said you might not."

Off in the woods, several hills over, two coyotes howled.

Primal, Joe thought. Their ancestors must have sounded that same way a thousand years ago. Sixteen years ago, there were no coyotes around Ellenton. They were claiming to belong. Maybe they did—smart enough to survive, proof enough of belonging.

"She told you?"

"Me, Hank Atkins, couple others." Harve pulled a cigarette out of the pack with his lips. "She wanted us to make it hard for you—something about you doing your best work in a challenge."

"She was a love constrictor," Joe said, remembering the morning at breakfast Libby had pounced on him from behind. "Like hugging a crocodile," she'd said, wrapping her arms around his neck. "I'm going to cut off your air supply with a love constriction."

"A what?" Harve said.

"Never mind. Not important."

Let's make it official," Harve said, picking up a piece of cedar. He pulled out a lighter and held the flame to the end of the splinter. The cedar flared then went out.

"Wait," Joe said, pulling himself up on what was once a fender. "Should be me."

Joe wondered if Libby had really told Harve that Joe would not be able to go through with it. Sounded like her. He wanted to ask Harve if Libby had called Wink, but decided he'd rather not know. Likely, it was part of her scheming, having Harve show up to light her pyre, prompting Joe to intervene. It didn't matter. It didn't even matter that it didn't matter.

Joe took the lighter and piece of cedar from Harve.

"I bought her first telescope," Harve said. "Shipped it to her from Japan."

"What was she like then?" Joe said.

"Pain in the southern end," Harve said. "A jabbering, star-gazing, eight-year-old pain in the ass."

"Then she's leaving," Joe said, "same way she came."

Joe lit the cedar, waited for the flame, then flicked it toward the barn. Before the fire ever touched the barn, things exploded, a cloud of flame sweeping around the structure. In minutes, flames engulfed the barn, then changed from yellow to orange, then to an orange so dark Joe had to squint to see it in the night. From orange, the flames turned red, then blue—a Caribbean blue. It was as if the Caribbean ocean had risen, shaped itself into a funnel. As the barn burned, the blue funnel grew tighter, the heat more intense. It reminded Joe of a tornado cloud, but so damn blue Joe and Harve shielded their eyes. The heat forced them behind the Subaru. Pine cones strewn about the yard ignited and their smaller blue flames were pulled through the air and into the funnel.

"Ever seen a fire burn like that?" Joe said.

"Fire does strange things," Harve said. "Ancient wood, soaked with who knows what." He lit a cigarette, took a draw. "And—"

Joe interrupted. "It's Libby." ■

THE BOX

We pick it out together, giggle uncontrollably over the
    pastel lining
the superfluous pillows sewn to the interior, deny
the shadow of cancer and fear that hides in the shadows
in the dark space between our palms when I take your hand.
I call you "Mom" more often now, forgo introducing you by
    first name
even to strangers. These last days, all I want
is for you to be my mother.

This seems a good enough place to bury your secrets
cushioned in unrealized dreams
of running away. This will be a place
where shouted orders aren't expected to complete you
where cracked pots and conceptual pieces aren't questioned
    on merit
where bluebirds come gift-wrapped
and sing only of self-preservation.

HOLLY DAY

CAVE OF FORGOTTEN DREAMS

After Werner Herzog

Four charcoal horses animate
in torchlight, that flickering first projector,
sans horsemen, pre-Apocalypse.
Red ochre palm print
by the cave mouth like a house number,
or graffito, preserved by landslide—
a human touch
kept from human touch
for 32,000 years,
the terms of ingress sealed
like a contract: We live
in peace, or want to.
Come and go in peace.

AMY WRIGHT

SEVEN-SECOND MEDITATION

Outside the window
a red-headed house
finch plucks seed
down from the grass
as if he is running late
for the theater, rifling
through the bureau
drawers, tossing scarves
over his shoulder, shells.

AMY WRIGHT

THE MINK

Each morning before school
she runs her father's traps,
a thirty-minute walk
along the creekbed
where darkness surrenders
to the cone of light
from her headlamp.

The mink she's caught
holds still in the snare
as she reaches into the backpack
for the .22 pistol that belongs
to her father, only to be drawn
if the pelt is worth killing for.

Danger, her grandfather says,
is peering into the eyes
of the animal you plan to shoot.
Simply place the muzzle
at the back of the skull
and squeeze the trigger.

She's felt the recoil
in her hand, like the shake
of muscle when she plays
with the rat snake that lives
under the porch. But before
she can click the safety off,
the mink's eyes pull her in,
until she stares out from a skull
that is not her own.

She's surprised not to feel fear.
Nor does she harbor hope.
A simple resignation to wait
for the bars grasping her leg
to open, that strange, toothless
mouth yawning in boredom.

She remembers what the mink
remembered: the comfort of water,
its song rubbing against stone.
If freedom finds her again,
she'll sing a hymn of thanks
to the moving current she's saved
within her chest.

When she was a girl she swam
in the quarry, diving from a ledge
into the sky's reflection.
That's what it's like inside this skull:
legs kicking deeper into a rock-cut pit.

And she wonders what the mink
must think of its new body,
the uprightness, the loss of fluidity,
but also the weight of that gun,
the decision whether to let her go
or to bring this body back
for her father to skin
and sell at market.

TODD DAVIS

LAST CHORES

My sons weigh more than I,

one measure of manhood.

They help me gather stone

to build with, wood to keep us

warm. Still a few apples

in the tallest branches. No need

for a ladder. I want the fruit

to fall in winter

when deer will draw back

their lips and gnaw.

First I'll till the compost,

sow some rye.

The blood-leaves

of tupelo

thresh the late

sunlight: veined,

every pulse slowing,

as we herd the long dimness

of approaching December

into the deepest part

of the hollow.

TODD DAVIS

BALANCE

MELISSA BALLARD

A frantic sound is coming from the laundry room. I drop the book I'm reading, race in, and open the aging pale-yellow washer that doesn't know how to stop itself. I redistrbute the clothes, shut the lid, and stand watch for a few minutes to make sure it stays balanced.

■ ■ ■

On a humid July evening, my mom, aunt, cousin and I are gathered in a hotel room in Tuscarawas County, Ohio, where all of us were born. I'm the only one who didn't grow up here. We are looking at stacks of family pictures. We come to a blurry black and white reprint. On the back, someone wrote, "Christmas Day, 1948." A tiny woman, head encased in a billowy white saucer of dust cap, stares from behind large, round glasses. She is neither smiling nor frowning. Seated alone on a sofa, she wears a forgettable dress, and her hands are folded in her lap.

"That's your great-grandmother, Minnie," Mom says. I've only heard of Minnie Mouse and Minnie Pearl, a comedian from the TV show *Hee Haw,* who always left the price tag on her hat. Later, I will find one document that reveals Minnie's full name: Wilhelmina.

Minnie died just six weeks before I was born in 1952, and she's buried not far from where we are sitting now. This is the first photo of her I've ever seen. Often, when I look at a family photo, I sense a connection to the person. Not this time.

We pass the photo back and forth, sip our drinks, and listen to the hum of the air-conditioning.

Mom: Well, she wore that dust cap all the time because she was bald.

Aunt: No, she wasn't.

Mom: She certainly was.

Aunt: No, she was not. I helped get her ready for her funeral and she had a full head of hair.

I want to scream. I couldn't care less if Minnie had hair or not. This is not why I study and write about family history. I want to know stories, to understand people.

I roll my eyes at my cousin, who tries to redirect the conversation: "We know her parents were German immigrants."

Slowly, we review all the research we've completed, which hasn't yielded much: Minnie had eleven brothers and sisters. Her father was a coal miner, who died when the youngest child was four. Minnie's mom never remarried.

Minnie married at eighteen on Valentine's Day; her first child was born soon after. She had three more sons, and then stopped eight short of her mother's offspring tally. Minnie was the mother of my beloved grandpa, the one person who was patient enough to sit with me hour after hour while I attempted to sound out words, slicing and dicing them into meaningless parts, then trying awkwardly and often unsuccessfully to put them back together. If she raised him, there must be something about her worth knowing.

■ ■ ■

On a Monday morning before work, I go to the dentist. He refers to me in the third person when speaking to his assistants, lamenting the fact that I can't keep my mouth still long enough for him to make a perfect impression for a crown. More appointments are scheduled; I grind my teeth and am at risk of shattering the ones I haven't already damaged. As I walk to work, pelted by a late April sleet, I wonder how much of these dental fees will be out-of-pocket and why I didn't ask more questions. At my office, I hang up my wet jacket, wrap myself in a bulky sweater, shut the door, turn on music, and sob quietly.

Anxiety had made guest appearances in the past, but now she came to stay. Too many major life changes might have contributed: a change in my job, with much more responsibility; my husband's retirement; my daughter's graduation from college and move out-of-state; my mom's increasingly delicate health.

I begin to wake daily at 3:30 a.m., my core painfully contracted, my limbs jittery and disconnected. My thoughts spin out of control. I imagine potential disasters and how they might play out: I would forget to turn off the stove and burn down the house. I would cause a major traffic accident. I would fail to submit grades and lose my job. The list is endless, and I am unable to get back to sleep.

Most people weren't aware of my anxiety. To those closest to me, I might have seemed self-absorbed. And I was, but only in the sense that I was terrified of making mistakes. I lost my sense of humor, which had always helped me when I felt awkward or inadequate.

I went to my doctor, who suggested therapy and prescribed daily medication which made me tired and lightheaded, but still anxious. I stopped taking it and tried an over-the-counter supplement that seemed to help. A therapy virgin at fifty-six, I began to attend weekly sessions. My goal became getting through the work day. I went home, did any necessary chores, and sat in front of the television while drinking wine. I watched the entire *Gilmore Girls* series multiple times, happy to escape into the weird small-town life of Stars Hollow.

I finally told my mom what was going on. She didn't acknowledge that I'd gone to therapy. For all I knew, I was the first person in our family to do so. We never talked about these things. After a long pause, she said, "I hope your doctor can fix it." We never mentioned "it" again.

I walked three miles most mornings, using the treadmill in the basement if I was not able to get outside. I also began to meditate, but sometimes I felt *more* anxious after I meditated. The therapist I saw suggested I try Sudoko; I told her I preferred crossword puzzles. "You need to do something that doesn't involve words," she said. They seemed to help.

Most Sundays, I never left house. I read novels, took naps, and wrote. And I got a different dentist.

■ ■ ■

I continue to write whenever I have time and energy. I take summer writing classes. I look forward to retiring, so I'll have more time to write. I don't know yet whether it helps my anxiety or makes it worse. I remember my mom telling me, when I was a child, that people who thought too much "lost their minds." When we drove past Massillon State Hospital, originally known as Massillon State Hospital for the Insane, and I stared at the turrets of the looming brick buildings, I tried not to think so much. Sometimes there were patients walking slowly along the paths. I wondered if they were looking for their lost minds.

I keep coming back to my notes about Minnie. I call my mom. "I need to know more about her. What was she like? What do you remember about her? "

After a long conversation, and some follow-up e-mails, I have this: Minnie was small but feisty. She kept her house spotless, scrubbed the woodwork until all the paint was gone, boiled the laundry. She bargained with the butcher for the best cuts of meat. She ate every meal at the dining room table, on a tablecloth she had washed, starched and ironed herself.

Minnie wasn't social, not a churchgoer, didn't go out much, didn't drive, she loved to listen to baseball games on the radio. When angry, she could "burn the ears off a truck driver" with a string of German curse words.

I search an online newspaper database. There are eleven matches for Minnie's name. Most are obituaries of family members, and two are about her own death. On February 18, 1931, Minnie made the New Philadelphia *Daily Times* when she injured her left hand in the wringer, sometimes called the "mangle," of her electric washing machine.

I imagine this tiny, sturdy woman in her billowing dust cap, darting quickly from one household chore to the next, the scent of bleach in her wake. And I hear her, hands fisted at her side, as she curses at the grocery delivery boy for bringing her inferior produce.

I type up my new notes. As I reread them, I underline phrases: didn't go out much, scrubbed the woodwork, boiled the laundry. My twenty-first century mind translates: depression, anxiety, agoraphobia, OCD. I think of all the things I've been doing to recover my mental balance, and I wonder how Minnie coped.

■ ■ ■

I retired. I began to build my days around exercise, meditation, reading and writing. These things made me feel better, and I now I had time for them. I thought anxiety had decided to leave me alone, or at least sit quietly next to me.

Nearly a year later, I got a new car. It had a keyless ignition. Every time I sat down in it, I had a panic attack.

My doctor helped me try a new medication. As soon as we established a therapeutic level, I began to notice a difference: I could drive without being terrified. I slept at night, and woke up without that feeling of dread. When I sat down each morning with a cup of strong, black coffee, I looked out the window at the seasons. I loved all of them, especially spring, with its lush lilacs and clusters of birds at the feeder.

I began to look forward to both time alone and social events. My sense of humor came back, and my husband and I joked that I was "Jimmy Buffet mellow."

■ ■ ■

My washer finally needs to be replaced. The new one occasionally starts to do the off-balance dance but it quickly stops itself. A soft chime goes off and a digital readout reports, "UE" (uneven). I move the clothes around and watch it resume its cycle.

I imagine Minnie standing to my right, in housedress and dust cap. She peers at the machine. Her eyes are huge behind her round glasses.

"Fancy, schmantzy," she says. "But does it get the clothes clean?"

I laugh. I won't even try to explain cold water settings.

I put my arm around her, and say, "Minnie, did you too savor the spicy-sweet scent of lilacs and the morning's first sip of strong black coffee? Wake up before dawn most mornings, your heart in a fist?" ■

BECOMING LADIES

They passed down the hush they remembered from
childhood, each generation of breasts and
feet forced into propriety until
they no longer knew who they were apart
from what they should not be, that list feeling
endless but which was, in truth, short: drawing
attention to yourself is impolite,
wait to be told what to do, freeze out the
reckless and indiscreet who can't control
themselves, always smile even when it's strained.

SANDRA KOLANKIEWICZ

JAMES BROWN PERFORMS "COLD SWEAT" ON AMERICAN BANDSTAND, 1968

We were practicing our splits, perfecting our slides
across the basement floor on one foot, impossible
to beat the hardest working man in show business
even as we cheated in our sock feet. Upstairs,
our grandmother hurled her wrecking-ball voice
at us before we finished miming the first verse—

I don't care *ha!* about your past
I just want *ow!* our love to last *huh!*

We knew she wasn't really hollering about the TV blaring
or that we'd skipped our Saturday housework chores.
She wasn't really cross that we dragged her white
chenille bedspread downstairs so we'd have a royal
robe to throw off at the end of the song. We twisted
against the timbre of her rage, while we mimicked Soul
Brother No. 1 cloaked by Danny Ray then coaxed
off the stage exhausted only to revive, abandon
the cape, grab that microphone and whirl
and gyrate and split
us one more time.

MARIANNE WORTHINGTON

PHOTOGRAPH

An American boy stands in front
of a Japanese flag, its red dot glowing,
the only color in the photo. The boy loved
his grandfather who hated all things
Japanese. The grandfather will not
buy the church a new piano,
even though he can,
because the church wants a Yamaha
or a Kawai. There's a committee.
The boy wants to learn to play
the piano, more than baseball, more
than He-Man, more than girls. A woman
in the church could give him lessons
but *not on no Jap piano,* his grandfather says
as if the keys were ground from bones,
as if the strings were cut from guts,
as if the harp would echo his screams.

MARIANNE WORTHINGTON

IN THE BEGINNING

The child dreams her mother as angel, cherub featured,
broad-faced, wide eyes, ginger curls— A nightlight

in the nursery brands shadows on the ceiling. Mother-
angel glides back and forth over the dreaming

child's crib singing coos and cradlesong. The child
cannot hear the tune the child never forgets

the dream the dream transfigures to myth the myth stirs
the holy spit and glue of memory benevolent
and dreadful as an angel.

MARIANNE WORTHINGTON

AN *APPALACHIAN HERITAGE* INTERVIEW

CHARLES DODD WHITE

"I'm trying to show characters that endure despite terrible things that happen to them," says Charles Dodd White about his most recent novel *In the House of Wilderness*, published by Ohio University Press in 2018. Striking a balance between darkness and beauty, between violence and joy, the novel brings to life a band of hippies, a college professor, and a photographer whose images have made a splash in the art world. All the while, White asks hard questions about Appalachia, examining the way two characters cope with both wilderness and wildness—and how they ultimately find each other in times of tribulation.

As with his novels *A Shelter of Others* (2014) and *Lambs of Men* (2010), as well as his short story collection *Sinners of Sanction County* (2011), *In the House of Wilderness* finds White unafraid to push boundaries in his writing. He recently spoke to *Appalachian Heritage* about the challenges of writing photography on the page, his views on environmental issues, and the inspirations for his recent novel.

■ ■ ■

EMILY MASTERS: Photography plays a major role throughout the narrative of *In the House of Wilderness*. Which Appalachian photographers were most inspirational to you during your writing process?

CHARLES DODD WHITE: Inspiration can be such a tough thing to define. In a way, pretty much every picture I've ever seen about Appalachia figured into the composite that Liza Bryant [from the novel] eventually became. One of the central concerns I had was exploring what it means to use something or someone as a means of making an artistic statement. So, it's impossible to think of something like that without Shelby Lee Adams coming to mind. I remain ambiguous in my own reaction to much of his work, though it's impossible not to recognize its artistry. But I'm also aware of the good and striking work of some contemporary photographers like Roger May, Rob Amberg, and Stacy Kranitz. I'm lucky enough to call Roger and Rob good friends, and I think the world of Stacy's work, though I've only talked to her a couple of times across social media. If I were to step beyond the strict influence of Appalachia, I'd say Sally Mann would be another person at the top of the list.

In terms of why I attach to them as touchstones, I think it's part of my fascination I have with people who follow artistic pursuits outside of writing. I'm interested in how they use a completely different but still recognizable language to get after the big concerns of life, death, love, and loss. I feel like I learn more about the person behind the camera each time I really spend time with their pictures. That's likely my projection, of course, and probably sounds more grandiose than I mean it to.

EM: What were some of the challenges you faced in describing photographic images on the page, in translating their essence to readers so they would be able to recreate a photograph in their own minds?

CDW: It can be a real balancing act. You want to convey without belaboring. Really, I think I end up seeing the emotional response of the characters being the engine that drives the rendering. If you were to try and capture all the ineffables of visual art, you would end up writing yourself in circles and certainly end up boring the reader. But if you can show some essential relationship between subject and object happening in the text then maybe the reader can become more tuned in to their own subject/object relationship they're having with the book they're holding in their hands. If that happens, the reader will remember the emotional narrative the image communicates.

EM: In one scene of your novel, you choose to reference *Deliverance*, one of the most controversial films about

the Appalachian region, in a positive light. Knowing how controversial the film's representation of the region is, what made you decide to include it?

CDW: I don't remember being particularly positive or negative, but I think it has been such a lightning rod for Appalachian scholars for the last several decades that any response to it other than condemnation might be viewed as decidedly favorable. It's such a huge piece of the American imagination about what Appalachia is that it's taken on a kind of hyperreality, and I think if you're going to talk about image and identity in the region as created by artists (in this case twofold, since both the [James] Dickey novel and the [John] Boorman film adaptation are about the region). Although I understand and agree with much of the criticism of the story as it constructs old tropes of the inbred hillbilly killers, it remains an excellent novel. The scene when Ed climbs the

Charles Dodd White

cliff face with his bow is one of my favorite scenes in fiction. And the film still has the ability to surprise contemporary audiences with its building menace. I think it would be a mistake to jettison it from what we consider worth our attention as Appalachian writers and thinkers.

EM: When a couple of the characters are street performing as stereotypical hillbillies in Asheville, North Carolina, to make a little cash, the scene feels reflective of the rise of the tourism industry in Appalachia, especially in places like Gatlinburg. What do you think about people in the region championing stereotypical behavior for their own financial benefit?

CDW: I'm not a big fan. There's this idea out there that a single act, whether it be a song or a dance or a picture or a book, that there aren't consequences to portraying characters like they don't matter. Poverty porn, I guess is a way of thinking about what I'm trying to say. Well, there are consequences. Each time you put your words or your images out in the world, your voice is amplified and that means a certain ethic needs to be considered. If you are lucky enough to have people listening to things you come up with then you owe it to your characters to get things right because if you're working right those characters come from your idea about what people truthfully are.

EM: In the novel, you write about a lot of touchy subjects including environmental issues, polygamy, police corruption, abortion, and adultery. Since wilderness is a major theme throughout the book, I found your meditation on disappearing wilderness especially interesting. On page 199, one of the main characters

meditates, "He wasn't exactly sure when it had happened, but a spirit of resignation had settled over those who had once been so ardent to defend the integrity of the natural world." This line seems like one of the darkest in a novel filled with violence in various forms. Does this reflect your beliefs about the wilderness, especially that in the Appalachian region?

CDW: I don't know. It depends on the day and that largely depends on how much of the previous night I sat up unable to sleep because I was worrying about whether humans are ever going to become serious about the world dying. I struggle with where we are in the natural world. I've never been famous for my sunny disposition to begin with, but the many environmental failures in the last few years coupled with the realization that things are probably much worse than we initially believed, makes me fearful in a way I wasn't even five years ago. There are some brighter patches like the fact that forestation seems to be consistently if slowly growing in North America, but the larger picture is grim. I think of books starting to be published now like William Vollman's *No Immediate Danger*, David Wallace-Wells' *The Uninhabitable Earth*, and Paul Schrader's film *First Reformed*, and how they point toward a new kind of environmentalist work. The kind that grapples with the heavy deed of what we have done and how we may be facing something beyond our ability to overcome.

EM: You strike a delicate balance between the darkness and the beauty of the human experience, the Appalachian experience. Do you see yourself as an activist through your writing?

CDW: I think that I'm trying to show characters that endure despite terrible things that happen to them. I hope that their actions carry weight for the reader. As corny as it may sound, I still believe that the act of writing novels can be a revolutionary practice. So, I would like to believe that my work is pointed in the direction of a philosophical good. I think that if we want our world to improve then it has to come from a place of imagination. Fiction is slow and small but it is an insistent factor in how a society tells the story of itself.

EM: What inspired you to write *In the House of Wilderness*? When the writing got tough or you felt like you were hitting a wall, what did you turn to for motivation or further inspiration?

CDW: I was interested in a story about two characters (the widower Stratton and the young woman Rain) both trying to escape something. In the case of Rain it was a literal wilderness that is the setting of her abuse at the hands of the man who calls himself Wolf. Stratton's wilderness is more metaphorical in that it is how I conceive of grief. So I wanted to see how these two people could mean something to one another and what that might say about their ability to heal.

As far as overcoming the blocks, there weren't any tricks. Just time in the chair and plain, old-fashioned obsession. ■

IN THE WEEPING SIFT

Growing up, a picture hung
above your tub

that probably haunts
every small-town peddlers mall—

the profile of a woman
in her bath

claiming a warm one
cures all.

You'd say the same
of the ocean—

no illness outlasts
a longful soak.

Salt rids the body
of sickness.

■

Having walked from Kentucky
to this beach in Virginia

I stand now blistered
in the weeping sift

of low tide, let the sores
that are my feet bury—

as you would—completely
still, sinking deep into sand.

Just south of Richmond
I caught word

that you decided
to forego the feeding tube—

arranged to phone you
upon reaching the coast.

Though time takes no mercy.
And your hour struck—

leaving me lodged with guilt
and goodbye in my throat.

Here facing the seam
that stitches sea to sky,

having last missed the chance
to hear your voice,

I curse the lump
for years you kept secret—

in the same breath praise
you at ease alongside.

For no further the wither—
deep-set disease,

months spent in vain
fettered to machines,

no longer raised arteries
pumped full of ice—

no more fierce cries
for and at god.

An easy whisper
on the thin of a breeze—

steadying my sway.
As the wash of water speaks.

CALEB GILL

NOCTURE IN F MINOR, MINERAL RIDGE

Father finagled a used baby grand
to make amends—I see that now.
I thought it too big for our lives then,
but I was a child.

That first day, as in a trance,
Mother played a light ribbon of a song,
unspooled it in the air.
Chopin, she whispered.

Then *Stardust,* and *Summertime,*
The Maple Leaf Rag, and with a smile and nod,
my father's favorite,
a steady *Tennessee Waltz.*

I ran to the sound of her music
floating through the sprung screen door.
As I quieted to the couch she saw and with a flourish
up the keys, she laughed and played for me.

A conspiratorial *Side by Side*
a ghostly *Mood Indigo,*
Pennies from Heaven and her Methodist hymns,
and always—when I asked—Chopin...

she played him as a gathering storm,
delicate steps in a dark forest,

then two fists fighting up the keyboard,
to find a peace, of sorts, in soft single notes,
and silence.

PRESTON MARTIN

ODE TO AIMLESSNESS

JENNIFER McGAHA

I am not athletic in the traditional sense. I do not ski or snowboard or participate in any activities that involve a ball or other bouncy objects. However, I have always been fairly active, and for a number of years I ran regularly. I loved the catharsis that running brought—the total whiteout of the brain. When I was running, all conscious thoughts stopped, and when I was finished, I was spent, emotionally satiated, physically ravenous.

Still, my activity of choice has always been walking, not power walking or competitive hiking or any such complex endeavor—simply walking. Walking in town. Walking on beaches. Walking on trails. Walking up mountains. Any kind of walking. Walking is the perfect exercise for me because it requires no special skills or talents. You do not have to learn to do it or train to do it. You do not need special clothes or equipment. You just do it. In her groundbreaking 1938 craft book *If You Want to Write*, Brenda Ueland recognized the power of walking to soothe creative, angsty souls. She also said writers should spend time each day engaged in what she called "moodling."

"[T]he imagination needs moodling," Ueland said, "—long, inefficient, happy idling, dawdling and puttering."

When I first read this, I was delighted. The list of things at which I was inept often seemed staggering, but idling? Dawdling? Puttering? Finally, here was a concise list of all the things at which I excelled. Of course, Ueland was not the first or the last writer to appreciate the creative stimulus walking affords. Henry David Thoreau, William Wordsworth, Charles Dickens, Carl Sandburg, Wendell Berry, and, by God, my own literary and walking heroine Cheryl Strayed all found solace and renewal in the outdoors, in "purposeless" strolling, if you will. For me, the walking came first, and the writing came later—much later.

Taking leisurely walks was a habit I developed early in life, one I inherited from both my parents. When I am walking, I can relax. The swirling thoughts that normally keep me agitated and anxious fall neatly into a logical sequence. I resolve problems with my writing. I prepare for my classes. I figure out what I want to say in a manuscript critique. I plan my weekly dinner menu, mentally compose a shopping list, untangle a tangled relationship. Daily walking gives me clarity and keeps my anxiety and depression at bay. If only I walk far enough and long enough and fast enough, I can present myself to the world as a relatively together person. If I miss my walk, I am unable to function. I cannot sleep. I cannot stay awake. I have panic attacks. I can't focus to read or write. I can't remember anything. I can't compose an articulate sentence.

It seems I have almost always been this way. In 1974, when I was seven-years-old, my grandfather, brother, and I walked ten miles from my grandparents' home in Canton, North Carolina to Lake Junaluska just for the hell of it. My eleven-year-old brother planned the outing, and he did his best to persuade me not to go because he worried I would slow him down, maybe even wimp out before we even got a good start out of town. He wanted this to be a smooth operation, flawlessly executed, and in fairness to him, his concerns were not unfounded. I had a history of having the *most* major, *most* public meltdowns at the *most* inconvenient moments. But I had insisted, and finally, my brother relented.

We headed out, down the hill, past the paper plant where my grandfather worked, onto the highway. It was a sweltering July day, and we had no water, no snacks, just an end goal in mind—the gas station next to the lake. There we would refuel on soda and snacks, then call my grandmother from a pay phone to report our mission complete. Though my parents frequently took my brother and me walking in the national forest near our home, this was my first long adventure, and about five miles into our journey, I leaned against the cement barrier on the underpass of a bridge.

"I feel faint," I said.

Trucks whizzed past. The sun blazed down. I was weak and sweaty, my knees a mass of gelatin. I envisioned myself bravely telling them to go on without me, but we all knew that was not a good idea. The last time I had been left alone—a few weeks earlier when my mother had left for a few minutes to check on the progress of the house we were building a few miles down the road—I had run barefoot and crying into the middle of a busy two-lane road where a concerned construction worker had picked me up and driven me to the new homesite.

I was still sobbing when he pulled down the dirt road and dropped me off in what would eventually be our front yard. The house was just scaffolding then, and my brother and I loved to play there, running from room to room, claiming spaces for our own. I found my mother sorting through paneling samples in what would be our kitchen. The moment I saw her there, her dark hair curling against her suntanned cheeks, one sandal cast aside as she propped one bare foot on top of the other, I felt safe, protected, right with the world.

"You are never staying home alone again," she had said.

"You're such a baby," my brother said now.

My grandfather eased down beside me.

"She's all right," he said to my brother. "She just needs to rest a minute."

Eventually, I saw that he was right. My breathing slowed. The grey lines in my vision abated. My head stopped pounding.

"I think I can keep going," I said.

And before I could change my mind, my grandfather grabbed my hand and pulled me to my feet. He held my hand all the whole way from Clyde to the lake, and by the time we reached the gas station, I had gotten a second wind. I skipped into the store and pulled an orange Nehi from the cooler—a victory beverage. Despite myself, I had made it, and for the rest of his life, my grandfather told the story of that walk. He told it at Thanksgiving and Christmas and Easter, on my birthday and my brother's birthday and his birthday until it became a family legend, a tribute to my fortitude, my endurance, my stick-to-itness.

"Ten miles..." he would say each time in conclusion. "Ten miles and you no bigger'n you were."

I know that if I had not walked to the lake that day, my grandfather would have found something else to be amazed by, some other way of telling me how strong and capable I was. He was just that kind of a man. Still, in his version of this story, I was able to see myself as he saw me, someone tougher than I really was, someone worthy of admiration.

I have an even earlier memory of walking, though whether I really remember it or only the telling of it I cannot say for sure. When I was two years old, I was supposed to be napping, but I was not, and when my mother was busy hanging laundry

I stood outside the courts, my hands gripping the fence, my face shoved against the cold metal until, finally, my astounded father noticed and ran out to grab me.

on the clothesline outside, I climbed out of my crib and walked a half mile down a busy*ish,* two-lane road to the high school where my dad was playing tennis. I stood outside the courts, my hands gripping the fence, my face shoved against the cold metal until, finally, my astounded father noticed and ran out to grab me. As he carried me home, I fell asleep on his shoulder, and I was still asleep when he handed me to my mother who had never even noticed my absence. It was my very first solo outing.

My adult life has been filled with similarly spontaneous and frivolous wanderings, though now I almost always walk in the company of at least one dog. For years, our Corgi mix,

Julie, was my walking companion. She was sweet and gentle and eager to please, and she had one lame back leg that she kicked out every time she took a step. Even now, I can still hear the rhythmic tapping of her toenails on the pavement—tip, tap, kick, tap; tip, tap, kick, tap.

After Julie, my Lab, Hester, became my go-to walking dog. Hester loved walking as much as I did. She only refused to walk when she could hear thunder or anything that sounded like thunder, like fireworks or gunshots. Together, over more than a decade, we walked tens of thousands of aimless miles. Rarely did we *go* anywhere or *return* from anywhere. We simply meandered down sidewalks and over streams and along wooded paths. We walked in the Pisgah National Forest and at Lake Junaluska and along the Mississippi River. We walked when it was ten degrees outside and when it was a zillion degrees outside. We walked so much at the campground near my house that Hester learned which bathrooms I liked to use (i.e., the ones that were heated, the ones closest to the most fastidious campground hosts). She plopped down in front of said bathrooms and refused to move until I either went inside or, in the unlikely event that I did not actually have to go, until I pretended to.

Some days, when bystanders watched as Hester sat staring pointedly at the bathroom door, I said loudly, "It's okay, Hester. You don't have to use the restroom. You can just go out here on the ground."

I said it with a straight face, and Hester and I both thought it was hilarious. Now, however, Hester has gotten too old to walk. Her hips are bad, her hind legs weak. These days, rather than walking, she prefers to hang out on our front porch barking at the coyotes and bears she hears or imagines she hears, so I have a new walking companion, a beautiful lab-husky puppy named Pippi. Though she will never take Hester's place, already she is learning my routine. She knows where I stop for breaks in town, the direction I always go when I walk around the college, the water stops along the way. She knows where the white squirrels tend to congregate and that, if she is good and does not jump and bite me or thrash about on her back or bolt after the squirrels, she will get to dip in the creek twice, once next to the college gym and a second time near the track. She knows that I am scared to go in the windowless, concrete bathroom behind the old Silvermont Mansion alone, but she is scared of it too, so we compromise. She stands in the doorway while I hold her leash and talk to her while I pee. Then we both get the hell out of there before something terrible happens. *Jennifer and Pippi, the worriers.* Though I still have moments when I am afraid, I am no longer alone.

Pippi also knows the trails at DuPont, the ones I frequent, the ones I avoid, the way I always stop at the end of the airstrip and sit a while. She knows that a spillway means a lake nearby, that wild turkey frequent the hillside near the Airstrip Trail, that large groups of mountain bikers are to be avoided at all costs. She knows that if a friend goes with us, she may get to go to Oskar Blues for a beer and a black bean burger, or at least to watch me have one while she gets the occasional French fry. It is enough, it seems, to keep her ridiculously happy, leaping in the air, smiling, all four paws off the ground.

Recently, an acquaintance in her early seventies told me that the most recent puppy she had gotten, a lovely, wild yellow Lab, would likely be her last. After this one, she would be too old to raise another rambunctious puppy to adulthood. Until that very moment, it had never once occurred to me that I might one day no longer be able to properly care for a dog or to take a walk. Somehow, despite the fact that I had watched both of my grandparents become fragile and frail in their later years, I had held onto the illusion that I might remain the same as I am now before simply dropping dead one day. I had not considered the dying itself, the weeks and months and maybe even years when my legs would become unsteady, when my vision would dim, and my hearing would weaken, and I would simply fade and fade and fade. And this would be if I was lucky, a best-case scenario.

Still, I know that even then, even after I am old, not just middle-aged but really old, I will dream of walking. I will sit in my soft-backed chair, a blanket folded over my lap, a pillow behind my back, dozing on and off, dreaming both when I am awake and when I am asleep. In my dreams, all the dogs I have ever loved will be alive once more, vital and vibrant and whole. You will not be able to convince me otherwise.

Together, my dogs and I will stroll around my hometown—down Maple Street, around Grove Circle and through Sylvania. We will head down the hill toward the park, circle the college, pause beside King Creek before climbing Jailhouse Hill and heading back to town. We will amble along the wooded path beside the Davidson River, circle Lake Junaluska, mount the hill to Connemara, Carl Sandburg's home. We will hike through Pink Beds, to Twin Falls, to Graveyard Fields, Sam's Gap, Black Balsam. From the top of Tennent Mountain, we will lean into the wind. On John's Rock, we will close our eyes and listen to the hawks circling overhead, to the powerful whooshing of their wings.

At DuPont State Forest, we will balance on rocks in Reasonover Creek, lean back on the dock at Lake Dense, our faces turned toward the sun. We will swim with schools of fish and snapping turtles in Fawn Lake. At the end of the airstrip, we will pause to look over the end of the mountain, the end of the world. We will hear Bridal Veil Falls in the distance, see the outline of the land below, imagine who came before us, where else we might go.

Always, my dogs will be with me—a Corgi with a stiff back leg, a yellow Lab with soulful eyes, a feisty Jack Russell, Frisbee-catching, man-wary Border Collie, a sweet but skittish Beagle mix, a demanding and determined Dachshund, a fierce and loyal Carolina dog, a scrappy terrier mix with a soft heart, a jumping, biting, life force named Pippi, and all the dogs from my childhood—Scotch, Snuggles, Pebbles, Shadrack. And when this life is over, my spirit will be free to roam these mountains with my dogs, to gasp in amazement at how swiftly and surely and wondrously this life has passed. ■

ALMANAC

I was the child in the dusk who heard her mother's voice as it arched across the house, became a background like the sizzling of power lines or sprinklers in the heat. I kept riding my bike, jumping sidewalks and banks. Flat-out lied when I came home and said, *I forgot the time*. That wasn't the only lie. I wasn't a child when my grandmother said on her porch, my halting place: *I was never in love with him*. Matter-of-fact, words as steady as her ritual of watering the flowers in the evening. I had been the one confessing, rattling on at twenty like my childhood bike chain. To sit and talk of *my friend*, never uttering the word *boy* when all I'd ever wanted to say was the scent-skin-tense of women. An erasure of boy had not been my first failure of language, the first time I laughed and talked to hide my tears. Call it a coming out foretold by the begonias and petunias, witnessed by my grandmother. So when I asked about her marriage to a man, how else could she respond? Who knows how she loved him. I only know how she loved me enough to slant the truth.

SUMMAR WEST

COKER CREEK

Calls to me along highway sixty-eight's
        signs for the Lost Sea
and the stretch of rambling on
        about relatives dead and gone,
the long inquiry about the kingdom of heaven.
        Look, up ahead on the *mountain*—
the place my grandmothers are from—
        always at a distance
always a visit.

Come over Unaka,
        come over Cataska,
go back to the timber
        clear-cut for decades
on Cherokee land.
        Let the record show:
Chera courses through
        all the roots
and veins and names.

This is one more place granted
        to white men after the Revolution
a lineage of soldiers and squatters
        preachers and moonshiners
Saturday nights and Sunday mornings.
        But it was a woman
who rode over five hundred miles
        by mule to fetch the deed.
I go after you, Pollyanna.

Legend says white men found gold
when a woman let the secret
slip during a dance.
Why is the most dangerous
place on a map
a woman's mouth?
So begins another obsession
with extraction.

Whipporwill
Yellow Dog
Hotwater
Calf Yoke
Paris
Underwood
Annette
for all the longing.

Witness once told me
great-great-aunt Cyn
went to the mines by night
panned for gold by day
to feed her family.
I think about their hunger
as endless as coal-black night or the shaking
of silt back and forth in a pan.

I think about more removal than gold.
Cherokee marched from their home,
how their bodies
made the Trail of Tears.

I can point where on a map
    of erasures or we can take
John Muir trail to the falls where Legend
    says a Cherokee princess comes and goes.

I'm nearing an end
    though I've only begun
to dredge like Cotton does
    when he's in the creek beside
my parents' house.
    Now tell me your Coker Creek,
the water where you cannot stay
    and the alluvium you cannot leave.

SUMMAR WEST

BONE BRUSH

Feathering away at the skin over your ribs while you sleep on top of me still so small as to be barely here—not like a house or a tree. Sometimes you hide and the only way I can find you is your eventual desire to want to be found. I imagine I'm sweeping away even that to the small braid of your being—in you a meaning I'm eager to grasp for both our sakes since you've been asking and telling me how afraid you are to die. I tell you what I've heard and what I hope is right that you will live a long life and death will be careful with you, not painful, slowly eroding you, untying the bow that anchors you here, a slow drift across a sky you find friendly and expectant.

CHRISTOPHER McCURRY

SMART HOUSE

KATHRYN MILAM

Maxine knows there'll be trouble the minute she sees the black bear roaming her front yard, a shadow in the drab morning light. It's small, a youngster, with a chest blaze, and it munches from an ash bush still laden with late fall berries.

Thirty-six years on this earth, in these mountains, and she can count on one hand the number of occasions bears have crossed her path. And every time, something bad has happened.

She cinches her robe tighter. That cold front promised by the weather forecast slipped in overnight from Tennessee. Snow stipples the hemlocks and the curled leaves of the rhododendrons. Flurries frisk in the wind, sprinkle the bear like confetti. Fall and winter are Maxine's least favorite seasons. The sadness of short days diminishes her.

She stokes the wood stove in the living room and starts the coffee pot.

■ ■ ■

When she was six-years-old, living here in the cabin her grandpa built, tucked away in a hollow twenty minutes outside of Boone, a female bear with two cubs circled the house before heading to Phipps's Creek, down the far property line in the back. She watched from the screened porch as they splashed in the pools below the rocky falls and thought they were the cutest things. That afternoon at school, she fell off the jungle gym during recess and broke her right arm in two places. The pink cast, speckled with glitter, stretched from her wrist to her shoulder. "Pink for a girl," the doctor said, though Maxine had asked for purple.

When she was twelve, another bear, his face aged to a sterling sheen, came right up on the deck while Mama cooked supper, pressed his nose to the kitchen's sliding glass door. He stared with moist, brown eyes, swung his shaggy head back and forth, then, after a while, lumbered on up the mountain. Maxine thought he seemed hungry and lonely, but Mama told her it was dangerous to feed wild animals. "He can take care of himself," Mama said. The next day, her daddy packed his old green duffle bag and left home for good, taking with him the two-toned F-100 Ford pick-up Maxine loved as well as her young heart.

Then, when she was fifteen-and-a-half, almost sixteen, and supposed to be working at McDonald's, saving for the college education Mama was determined she'd have, she went out riding with Henry Barclay instead. Henry was twenty-two, and he knew things she didn't. They came up on a huge male right in the middle of Shulls Mill Road, and they would've hit him if Henry hadn't veered onto the shoulder toward a steep incline that sloped toward the Hound Ears Golf Course. Maxine figured they were goners for sure, shouted "Jesus," felt a jolt of prayer coming on that God would forgive her sins and that she'd see her grandma in heaven. But Henry was a good driver. He swerved back in his lane at the last second and cruised on down the road like they were out for a Sunday drive. Maxine let her prayers slide away.

A couple of days later, she told Henry she was six weeks late and that a baby was surely on the way. She imagined they'd marry, set up an apartment in town. She could add shifts at work until Henry could get a job of his own. Mama wouldn't like it, sure. Still, Maxine daydreamed about blue-flowered dishes and a yellow couch, a nursery papered with Disney characters. But she never saw Henry again. He up and joined the Army that next week and was killed on his second tour in Afghanistan when little Ethan was not quite two years old.

Yes, bear sightings mean tribulation, no question.

■ ■ ■

Maxine keeps her eye on the bear, glances out one window then another. She pulls on khaki pants and the white shirt with *Maxine* embroidered in red across the pocket. The bear saunters toward the house, stops near her blue work van with "Mountain Alarm: Smart Homes for the High Country" painted on the side. He rises on his hind legs, sniffs the air, and Maxine is certain he winks one eye at her. Finally, he lurches across the road that runs close to the house and sets off into the woods. Tree limbs, a few brittle leaves clinging to their last hope, tremble as he passes. Then he is gone.

She searches once again for the earring she lost the night before. She's sure she had it when she got home from work, but she's already combed the kitchen, moving the knick-knacks Mama left behind when she moved to assisted living. They crowd the green Formica counters in little flocks. Maxine doesn't have the heart to get rid of them, though tidiness is one of the few ways she keeps herself calm.

All her life, Mama collected chickens, roosters, too, and there must be a hundred of them, all shapes and sizes and colors, small ones lined up on the mantel, big ones holding open doors. Maxine boxed up a few and took them to the Mile High Senior Living Center where Mama's been since her stroke, an event that left her confined to her bed or strapped in a wheelchair, one or the other.

A stroke sounds like a pen marking paper or the flick of a brush through hair. But this kind of stroke—it's more like a complete transformation of a body, cells replacing cells, papery new skin slinking over the old, a heart that's forgotten how to pine. This woman is a whole other person who isn't her mama at all. Yet Maxine keeps her trinkets.

The Mile High folks allowed her to leave only one of the chickens, a wooden, blue-painted bird on a stick that looks more like a cartoon seagull standing on one leg. Maxine set it on the bedside table, and Mama lifted a hand to it. One side of her mouth hoisted into a smile, and silently, she moved her lips as if to say *hello, chicken, I'm happy to see you,* which is more than she ever does when Maxine visits.

■ ■ ■

The earring isn't in her bedroom, not ground into the carpet or dangling from the red sweater she'd slung over a chair. She can't find it in the bathroom, and it's not in the living room, lost among the couch cushions.

If it were just any earring, Maxine wouldn't worry so much. The little bit of jewelry she owns isn't worth finding. But these were a gift from Ethan, his last gift. Truth be told, his only gift to her since the macaroni Christmas ornaments and watercolor Mother's Day cards he made in elementary school, those things tucked away in a plastic box under her bed along with trophies from two years of Little League and report cards, kindergarten through twelfth. Ethan had shown promise. His teachers said so, right in the glowing comments typed after every grading period. But he hadn't lived up to it, the promise. Twenty-years-old and he's not once thought about college or much of a job, at least as far as she knows.

She scans the kitchen, looks for a flash of metal, moves chickens, pokes in the garbage. These earrings, beautiful and sparkly, are gold-plated with dangling chains, each holding a colored stone, turquoise, red, yellow. They gently bat her neck when she moves. Ethan brought them to her after being gone from home for three months, God knows where and without so much as a phone call. Oh, she'd looked for him, high and low. Called friends she knew of, checked at the Hot Cross Coffee Bar where he once worked, even asked a guy at the sheriff's department if he'd heard anything. But, no. Just some mention of Asheville, possibly, maybe. Then, one night, late February, about a year ago, when she'd just about given up faith that he would ever return, he stunned her, crept through the front door, ambling in like nothing had happened, like he'd been out for a night in the bars or on the slopes with his snowboard, plaid shirt filthy, mud splattered on his jeans up to his knees, his frizzy yellow hair twisted into mats. He smelled of liquor and cigarettes and, oddly enough, cat urine.

"A little present, Mama," he said and dropped a silver box in her lap before turning around and walking right back out again.

She watched him fade into the night, get in the passenger's side of a beat-up car, blue, maybe red. It took off in a spin of gravel, tail lights disappearing around the bend toward Foscoe. She didn't get a good look at who was driving, and she stopped herself from running down the road flailing her arms after him. He seemed like a boy who didn't want to get caught, especially by his mama. He'd come back when he was ready. She knew he would.

But he didn't. That night was the last she saw her son alive. A college kid catching an early ride to class found him at a bus stop in Boone the next morning, frozen to death in a brutal cold snap, packets of crystal meth in his pocket, so the cops said. That's the way it is with methamphetamine addicts, they said. When they come off a high, no matter where they are, they just sleep and sleep and sleep, a sleep befitting the dead. Where Ethan got the money for drugs, Maxine didn't know. She was sure of one thing though. He'd stolen those earrings.

■ ■ ■

Maxine leaves the quiet of her cabin behind and drives her truck up the mountain to Buzzard's Roost to her only job of the day. It's a big one, setting up everything from Wi-Fi to video doorbells and various devices, all in one house, getting the whole place under control and impervious to intruders. Complicated work, and something she's proud she can do. She gets a commission on everything she installs, a fat check for this project.

She started with Mountain Alarm in June, gave up her longtime job as day manager at the Meadowbrook Inn and Spa for something more lucrative. After four weeks of training, she's the best installer they have, and she's usually the tech who gets sent on the trickier jobs. She turns houses into smart homes. A lot of times, sketchy cell service makes installation impossible. Those folks have to settle for regular service through a regular phone, nothing smart about it. The nooks and crannies of the Blue Ridge block cell towers and houses below a ridge can just about forget it. Reception at her own home is weak at best though it's all she's got now. She ditched her landline to save a few bucks back when her mama first got sick.

She throws up her hand at a passing car and broods on the bear. An adolescent, she decides, not old enough, maybe, to be away from its mama.

Out on the road, light snow flits on her windshield. She throws up her hand at a passing car and broods on the bear. An adolescent, she decides, not old enough, maybe, to be away from its mama. It should be snuggled warm and sheltered in a den, waiting out the winter cold, like nature intended. But what does she know? She hasn't studied the habits of wildlife, no more so than anyone who lives with the understanding that animals are just part of this territory. Youngsters like him, she figures it's a he, might be hard-headed, might steer his own course, forgoing the safety that seems so obvious to her. That might be what bears do.

The house, once she sees it, is even bigger than she's heard, an immense, glittering structure, brand-new, all glass and metal, perched on a cliff overlooking the valley and

Grandfather Mountain beyond. It'll take her the whole day and then some to set-up cameras and thermostats and alarms, all the technology controlled from a phone app that makes a house secure. But pre-wired, like most new construction. That's easier.

She skids on a patch of ice as she inches up the winding, asphalt drive, corrects herself just in time to avoid a stone wall encompassing a bank of hemlocks.

It's a vacation place, thank goodness, no one here during a cold week so near Thanksgiving. She'll not have some skinny brunette, dolled up in her supposed-to-be mountain wear, hanging over her all day, asking questions, making suggestions. As if she, Maxine, isn't the expert.

She pulls out the house key she won't need once everything's installed. When she's finished, the homeowners can unlock the door from anywhere in the world and let in her or the FedEx guy or the house cleaners, all the time watching on camera. It gives her the creeps, thinking someone might always have an eye on what she's doing. Still, she doesn't blame folks for wanting that peace of mind. It'll keep the bears out for sure.

Inside, the house is spectacular. Gleaming wood floors, a massive fireplace, soaring ceilings, a blue-lacquered stove that's the size of her kitchen. She opens her iPad and gets started.

■ ■ ■

Maxine finishes up at 4:30, long before she expected. She's that good at what she does. She chooses the long way into town, glimpses peaks glossed with snow, trees swaying in a light breeze. She contemplates the way the evening haze settles into hollows, creeping down into crags. Another freezing night, and sleet, if the weatherman's right. She imagines the bear from the morning, resting in the security of his den, fat and full of berries. She hopes that's where he is.

She ends up like she does every afternoon, where her mama lives—the Mansion, Maxine calls it, what with the big white columns out front and the curlicued Victorian benches on the porch. They've cleared the sidewalk, but snow still dusts the Fraser firs that flank the front door. A light sleet pings on the pavement.

The center isn't depressing at all. In fact, Maxine pictures herself here, being cared for, cooked for, not a worry in the world. The front desk always has a cheerful seasonal flower arrangement, and the nurses wear brightly colored scrubs and smile a lot. Now that she sold off her grandfather's hundred acres to Blue Ridge Development, she can afford the monthly charges. She hated to see the property go, but she's made herself satisfied with the cabin and the plot of land next to the creek and the good care her mama gets. She could buy a new car with what's left if she wanted, a nice four-wheel drive, good on mountain roads, or fix up the house, new paint, a new couch. But she doesn't really want new things, not anymore. Every now and then, she remembers the bear and the deer and the mink that live in those hills she sold and wonders what might happen to them when houses start going up. But she had Mama to think about, so what else could she do? Even with her good-paying job, Maxine could never afford this place.

"They got her out to the day room this morning," Robert, the custodian, tells her when she walks in. "I don't think she liked it much."

Maxine finds Mama sleeping in her room, feet poking up the covers like the twin mountains outside. She kisses her forehead and sits in the chair beside the bed to watch her for a while. Having seen the bear and all, she decided that her mama might die today. But here she is, breath still in her, heart still beating. Maybe the bad news was just the never-found earring.

"You have a good night, Mama." She cuts her visit short, hopes to get home before the storm starts in earnest. "See you tomorrow." She straightens the chicken, who gazes at her with a suspicious eye.

■ ■ ■

The last stop on her way home is the spot where Ethan died. It's become a ritual. Somebody hammered a wooden cross into the ground nearby and hung trinkets on it—a silver locket that glints despite the slate clouds, a string of purple and gold Mardi Gras beads, a bunch of fake yellow tulips. She sits in the van for a minute and lets the grief rise, and just as quickly, she shoves it away. She thinks of herself as a member of her own private club, AA for the Sorrowful, a place to acknowledge her pain, commiserate with herself. She admits she has no power over heartbreak then promises herself each evening when she's here not to indulge it. If you can make it through the day without a tear, then the deluge can't engulf you, she decided early on, and so far, it's worked. Mostly.

Her cell on the seat beside her rings.

"You coming tonight?" It's Raymond, one of the friends she joins every Tuesday and Friday at Bob's Beer and Bratwurst.

"Nah. Long day."

"Change your mind, we'll be there."

"Probably not." Maxine peers at the cross, jabs at the lump rising in her chest.

"You okay?"

"Yeah. Sure. I'll see you Friday if not tonight." She hangs up and nudges the truck onto the street, snatches one last glance in the rearview mirror at the cross and its decorations standing tall and alone.

■ ■ ■

Maxine takes the turn off 105 and heads east toward darkening sky on Poplar Church, a winding, but newly-paved road, with a hairpin curve that always sprays fear up the back of her neck. A grungy Toyota Corolla, red, parked on the shoulder pulls behind her and follows her van for a quarter mile before turning off on an uphill gravel lane. The car seems familiar, but she can't think where from.

Coming up on her house, Maxine keeps a watch for the bear in case he's decided to return to polish off the berries, but all she sees are a doe and a mostly grown fawn grazing in the horse pasture next to her property. The horses eat right alongside the deer, a happy conclave. Maxine enjoys imagining what kind of conversations they must have.

Inside, she flips on the TV to the local news, starts warming chicken stew for supper. The wind picks up. Another long night ahead. She thinks about the dead sweetgum off the porch and jots a note to remind herself to get somebody to take it down before it falls this winter and splits her roof. She's about as far away from a smart home as she can be, making notes on paper. When it comes down to it, she's old-fashioned like that.

She calls the Mansion, giving Mama one last chance to be the fulfillment of the bear sighting. Maxine lives on the edge, always expecting some trial even without bears. But Mama's fine. She's resting comfortably, they say. Ate a nice dinner. Tucked in for the night.

There's a knock at the door just as Maxine finishes washing up the dishes. She never gets unexpected company so she peeks out the window before letting in whatever riff-raff is stalking these hills at such a time. A car sits right at her front steps, the Corolla she saw earlier, and a man standing there, shuffling from one foot to another. To her surprise, she recognizes him.

"Johnny?" She opens the door to a boy who was her son's best friend since first grade. "What in the world?"

"Ms. Johnson. Just passing by."

"Well, come in out of the cold."

Maxine pulls him by a scrawny elbow. She'd know him anywhere, the eyes so like his Filipino mother, tall like his American dad. But he's thin, spare as a spindle, and that's different. He used to be fleshy and round, and if the kids teased him, it was for that, not for his sad puppy eyes.

"What in the world?" she says again.

"Hadn't seen you in so long. Thought I'd just say hello." Johnny drifts into the living room, collapses on the couch without being asked. He has a pungent smell, a whiff of ammonia, and the acne that plagued him as a young teenager taints his skin like scabs on an apple tree.

"Heard you'd moved to Asheville." Maxine takes the recliner she usually sits in when she watches TV. She can't think why this boy is here, now, when he didn't even show up at the funeral. She mutes the sound on an old episode of *Law and Order.*

"Don't let me keep you from anything," Johnny says. He's snatching at thick black hair that hangs rough to his shoulders, balling it in one hand and twisting it around his fingers. He rubs at a boil on his neck, and it starts to bleed.

"You okay?" Maxine wonders where she left her phone. She hasn't seen Johnny in two years, maybe more, and he's changed. She'd heard he moved for a job, and somebody said something about drugs. "You hungry?"

"Nah. You got money selling land, right?"

The stark question about money stuns Maxine, but Johnny's got the look—skinny, unwashed, desperation twitching the corners of his eyes—signs she should have noticed in Ethan but didn't.

"Some." She wonders if he plans to rob her or if it's just a handout he wants. "Mostly goes to paying for Mama's assisted living. You at your daddy's?"

The wind howls, and Maxine hears sleet pelting the tin roof. She considers shoving Johnny outside, handing him a twenty-dollar bill, which is all she has on her, and being done with him. But, he's pitiful, his brown eyes swollen and glassy, the blood and pus from the boil seeping into his shirt collar.

"You got a beer?" He wheezes, like an old smoker, his tongue licking the corners of his raw mouth.

"Sure." Maxine walks in the kitchen, eyeing Johnny all the while. He's stretched out with his sock feet on the coffee table, still plucking at his face and hair. Her phone isn't on the counter, not in the pocket of her jacket that hangs on a chairback, not on the windowsill where she sometimes puts it so she knows where to find it. She must have left on the dresser in the bedroom after she called the Mansion, but she can hardly go searching for it now, what with this kid lolling in her living room and her not wanting to alarm him. She notices the useless landline phone.

"Brought you some peanuts, too." Maxine hands Johnny the Heineken she buys when she has a little extra cash. "Eat something."

Johnny takes the beer and ignores the nuts, gulps long and loud. A snarl grinds from his throat, somewhere between a belch and a growl. He sets down the bottle and picks at his face, and now that's bleeding too. He's holding a pistol with a red grip in his lap.

"You got money?" Johnny clutches the gun and taps it on his leg. "You never did like me," he says.

Her chair is three feet away, and Maxine thinks if she can just get there, sit down, talk to the boy, reason with him, she can get them out of a situation that won't end well for anybody.

"Sure I like you, Johnny. What makes you say that?" She inches away from him, hears a scratching outside and thinks for a minute the bear has come back, not safe in his den after all. But it's just a tree limb scuffing at the window. All those alarms, all those smart houses she's set up, and here she is with no way to contact anyone unless she can find her phone.

"This here?" He waggles the pistol at her, then points it toward her belly. "This here I got for protection. Now, sit down. You make me nervous."

She inches away from him, hears a scratching outside and thinks for a minute the bear has come back, not safe in his den after all.

Maxine eases into the chair, focusing on his face. "You don't need protection from me."

"Sure I do. You always hated me." Johnny leaps off the couch, starts pacing back and forth in front of the fireplace. Embers in the woodstove whip up in a blaze with a gust down the chimney.

"Aw, Johnny. That's not true. You're one of my favorites. Ethan said that, too. He said you were the one he could count on."

Johnny whips around and stands over her, the gun aiming toward her forehead. "Liar," he shouts. "You and my daddy too. He don't want me."

The breath has gone out of Maxine. She gasps for a bit of air, tries to quell the panic in her gut.

"Let me help you with that sore. Your shirt's getting all bloody." Maxine thinks of Mama, her gaunt body warm beneath a fuzzy blanket, and is thankful she's not here for this. She wishes she were there with her, snuggled close, under the covers, not a bear or a deranged boy in sight.

The sleet pings harder, tapping at glass and tin. She pictures the bear busting through the door, breaking up this mess.

"Listen," Maxine says. "The storm. Let's get you cleaned up."

"No, no, no, no." Johnny howls like the gale outside, stomps and twists around the room. He swings the pistol in front of him, first toward Maxine and then toward the windows. "I'll shoot every one of them out. I'll shoot you."

"Come on, Johnny. You don't want to hurt me." The chair seems to seize Maxine's body. She couldn't get up if she tried.

"I don't, do I? I don't want to hurt nobody." The gnarl in his voice drops to almost a whimper. His frenetic march halts, and the spasms in his shoulders dwindle. Maxine thinks he might cry. He yanks at his hair again, pushes it back from his face. "I really don't."

"I can help." Maxine's heart pummels her chest and shifts toward her throat. "Ethan. He'd hate to see you like this."

Johnny flops onto the couch, the gun still hard in his hand. His eyes flutter like a sleepy baby's. "Ethan?"

Maxine's phone rings, the cheery *chirp-chirp-chirp* tone of crickets she never bothered to change. From the kitchen, it sounds like, lost amid a clutch of chickens. She moves to get it.

"Don't." Johnny flicks the gun at her, but she can tell his heart's not in it, and so her own heart soothes, slides to her breastbone.

His head slumps, eyes barely open. "My fault," he says. "Mine."

"What's your fault, Johnny?" Maxine scans the space between Johnny's drowse and the limp hand holding his weapon. She edges out of her chair. "What?"

"Ethan." Johnny squints. "I left him."

"Left him where, Johnny?" She slips closer, finally sitting next to him. His body's hot, like he has a fever, and the cat piss smell overwhelms her.

"At the bus stop. He got out of the car. Said he wanted to be alone. I didn't mean to." His words trail into gibberish, and he sinks, just like that, into sleep.

Maxine sits for a while, listens to the boy's jagged breath, studies his wasted face, wonders what kind of demon could have left her son alone like that to such a terrible death. The sleet's slacked off, but the wind continues its scream through the trees and roar down the chimney. Finally, she prods the gun from his hand and holds it, shelters it in her palm. She wonders if she could do it. Place the barrel to his side, pull the trigger, end his misery and appease hers in one furious rush. She strokes the grip. Who wouldn't believe that she, a woman alone, confronted by a raging drug addict, was simply defending herself?

Johnny's eyes quiver. He smacks his lips and throws one arm over his head, sinks deeper into the cushions. He breathes out a stench, the smell of dead carcasses.

Maxine watches him, doesn't sleep. She listens to the mantel clock tick the night away. The events of Ethan's life play in her head like a movie. The light outside brightens, and the new morning simmers in the eastern sky over Elk Knob, the storm passed into yesterday.

She stows the gun on the mantel behind a steely ceramic rooster, his tail feathers fluffed in a fan. She finds her phone, right on the kitchen table hiding beneath a dishtowel, and she texts a message to the office saying she's taking a sick day. The flu, she writes, something that might keep her gone for a while. Those homes can wait to become smart.

She covers Johnny with blanket, puts on a pot of oatmeal, and settles in to wait for him to rouse. She's read enough about meth to know his waking can go either way. Docile or angry. Pliant or aggressive. But she's in it now, and safety for both of them is on her mind.

From where she sits, she can see yesterday's bear return, rambling across the road, sniffing the brisk breeze. She worries he's straying from the protection of his den, lured by the sweet berries, distracted from the shelter he'll need to get through the coming months.

His presence doesn't bother her today though. She's not looking for trouble. She's formulating a plan, securing a quest in her mind that she's determined to win, something she could never do for her mama or her daddy or even Ethan.

Her earring's gone, but Johnny's here. And the bear. She's made up her mind, for once, that finally, she's the one who can beat the odds. ■

MY FIG TREE

Too tender for my climate, it seems, though Jim,
just a few miles away, grows them quite well.
I have planted mine on the sunny south side

of the house, the warmest spot I can find,
the most protected from the lethal winds.
Still, it has winter-killed for three years now,

dying back to the roots and forcing me
to cut it to ground level. I watch it
slowly grow to full height before it fruits—

fruiting so late the figs which do emerge
cannot ripen before the heavy frosts
of autumn kill all except three or four.

But it persists, and I persist, hoping
the weather gods give this tree softer days
and gentle nights, clement winds from the north—

just one good season of bloom, growth, and birth.
We are stubborn, we two, and we'll persist,
till one of us goes underground and stays.

DAVID BLACK

FRESH TRACKS

JONATHAN BURGESS

Dominik and I left the edge of our little suburban village and headed down a small dirt path for the woods, the smell of honeysuckle and magnolia growing stronger with each step.

"What kind of tracks do you think we'll see, Dad?" he asked, bouncing in slight zig-zags in front of me. The question sounded less like something he wanted to know—because he'd been studying a booklet of animal tracks and prints for months—and more like a way to chat with me. I smiled to myself.

"Oh, I don't know, buddy," I said. "There's a lot of construction out here now, stirs them up. This is our back yard, but it was theirs first. I imagine we'll see some coyote tracks. Probably some deer and maybe turkey."

He stopped fast and halt-turned back to me. His head was tilted down, corners of his mouth turned away from his wide hazel eyes. "Think we'll see some snake prints?"

Smiling, I kept walking to him and put my arm around his shoulders to bring him along. "It's springtime. They're out and about now. Where do you think they'd be?" I said.

"Well, they probably want to sun themselves. They want water," he said, eyeing the bushes at the edge of the path. We'd made it out of the neighborhood and into a grassy path surrounded by bright emerald shrubs and brown briar patches.

"They want water, but what else do they want near water?" I said. "What else comes out in spring?"

He looked up at me, a sharp swivel, and gasped. "They want food. Rabbits and mice and stuff come out for water, too. They're hunting," he said with a hint of satisfaction at remembering the answer.

I stepped ahead first and moved Dominik behind me as we carefully edged around a cluster of green and red-tipped thorns clawing into the path from either side. I was grateful I wasn't in the fields of Camp Pendleton, where I learned how to track. There, we called it the back yard too but with more sarcasm. It always reeked of sage—too strong, not like a pinch for food, but overpowering—and the bases of the tall, steep hills were always colder than the rest of the trail, especially just before dawn. I was grateful I wasn't in Afghanistan, where we tracked at night with a blue lens, trailing watermelon farmers and opium harvesters, looking for Taliban, creeping low and fast and silent between mud huts and clay compounds. I smelled sage and poppy and the heat pressed on me, pushed me down and out of the trail.

"What do snake tracks look like, Dad?" Dominik said. He stood farther down the trail, several meters away now, from where I stood staring into the waist-high grass ahead. The stems looked like poppy stalks, but when my stare reached the top, it just ended, a tapered blade of grass, no flower. I inhaled hard through my nose, breathed deep the honeysuckle and magnolia and looked up to the top of the tree line ahead. I could smell a hint of the pines now.

"Let's go around that grass, buddy," I said and walked to him. I ushered him through a right turn onto a small grassy pathway and aimed for the pines and elms surrounding the power company right-of-way on one side with a swampy river on the opposite side of the powerlines.

He gave a firm nod. "Good thinking, Dad. There are probably some snakes in there. What do their tracks look like? Are there different tracks for different snakes?"

"I'm sure there are, but I don't know them like I should. Don't they have them in that little booklet I got you?" I said.

He nodded and rummaged around in his cargo pockets and produced the white, weather-resistant, spiral-bound booklet of animal tracks and prints.

"This book has scat in it, too," he said with a mischievous smile. His two front teeth had grown in much larger than the others, and he had a habit of pressing them to his bottom lip, still getting used to his big kid teeth. He opened the book to show me a page with examples of various types of animal feces and giggled, the same kind of bouncing tense-necked giggle he had as a baby. I laughed too in spite of myself.

"Does it tell you if there are different smells for different scat, or does it all smell pretty much the same, all smells like chicken poop?" I said, laughing more. Dominik tossed his head back in laughter, too.

"I don't think so, Dad. You're silly," he said and kicked a bundle of yellow straw away from the path in front of him.

I tried to conjure smells of various animal poo, but I could only think of chickens. Southern Afghanistan was hot in the summer, and I had to sleep in a section of compound where the previous tenants still had several chickens. Fowl turds covered the hard-packed dusty earth, and in the ink-black night, I found a clear patch and bedded down on straw, sweating myself to sleep, exhausted from the day's fight. Short, light breezes swept the stench across the ground and into my face, but I was too drained to do anything but draw a

Short, light breezes swept the stench across the ground and into my face, but I was too drained to do anything but draw a shemagh *over my wet, dirt-caked face.*

shemagh over my wet, dirt-caked face. Just before I drifted off, I stole one last look at the laminated 3-D ultrasound picture of Dominik and imagined a Taliban grenade sailing through the open air over the compound wall landing in my straw bed.

"Dad, look!" Dominik called. He stood ten paces away pointing at the bank of a small still pond, tiny water skeeters skating across the murky brown and lime-green filmy surface. I was scared and a little embarrassed at how far away I had let him walk. I made up the distance between us with long, anxious strides.

"What is it?" I said.

"It's scat! What kind do you think it is?" he said.

I eyed the small, brown droplets. Each was tubular and seedy with blunt ends and irregular blobs.

"Probably a cat or a racoon," I said.

Dominik glanced at me and curled his lip.

"What's in it? Can we mush it with a stick and see what's in it? I bet we could figure out what they like to eat," he said and looked around for a suitable implement.

I laughed, forgetting the lapse a moment before, and Dominik laughed too, amused that I'd laughed about poking poo.

"No, buddy. Let's leave it alone," I said and walked ahead of him around the pond.

I motioned for him to come along, and he ran to my side.

"Do you know much about the spinosaurus, Dad?" he said from under the bill of his Marine Corps cap.

He scrunched his lips under his nose and narrowed his eyes at me, waiting. It was the type of esoteric eight-year-old-boy question rooted in wonderment he asked me often with a sincere expectation I had thorough, accurate answers for him. Though, I rarely had answers for anything.

Trying to parse the word out into something I could discern from mere linguistic morphology, I pulled him to me by his far shoulder and looked at the dirt path ahead of us. A three-foot viper stretched across the trail not two paces from us and the sight of it shot a slivering terror from my feet to my chest, tight from shoulder to shoulder.

"Stop!" I said, eyes wild.

I tore Dominik from the trail and shoved him behind me almost sending him stumbling into the pond to our right. I held my hand out behind me to keep him back and lifted one heel, ready to stomp the thing.

It didn't move.

I leaned closer and squinted at the snake. It wasn't the longest I'd seen in the wild, but it was thick like a flexed forearm muscle and tapered to a broad head and blunt snout. The mouth was open, jaw slack, with the head canted slightly, and the bright white inside contrasted with the charcoal and nut-brown color of the body, the tail a golden tip at the other end. It was the color of the sky minutes before the pitch of night smothered the last shades of dusk.

"Cottonmouth. It's a cottonmouth, Dad. Aww. It's dead," Dominik said, nose wrinkling as he showed his front teeth.

I nodded. "Yep, that's a cottonmouth. He's dead. Look at the tracks around the head," I said and pointed to the prints.

"What is that? A boar? No. Deer?" he said.

"It's hard to tell because of all the movement, but I think it's a heavy deer with a lighter, smaller deer close by," I said, following smaller, shallower prints closer to the brush.

"Maybe the mommy stomped the snake to death so he wouldn't bite her baby fawn," Dominik said, satisfied.

"Yeah. Maybe," I said and pulled out my cell phone and took a picture. "That's really interesting. Let's keep moving, though. See what else we can find."

I pushed my phone back into my pocket, put my arm around Dominik, and we continued on. Even moments later, my heart was still beating hard, pounding pulse in my ear. The seconds I'd thought the snake was alive and well I wanted to push Dominik far away from it, the terrible white flash of its mouth telling me it would be a nasty bite, too much for a small boy, my beautiful, smart, lively boy. Imagining the two puncture wounds on his leg, a past patient came to the front of my mind as we strolled through the dirt path and wound our way through the brush and into a clearing by the tree line.

A boy and his mother came into the ER after being attacked by a newly-adopted dog. They said it was a mixed breed adult male and didn't like it when they approached his food while he was eating. The boy, about Dominik's age, had forgotten and tried to pet him while he ate. The dog turned on him, the mother had said, latched onto his leg. Once he was on the ground screaming for his life, the dog began chomping both legs, then his arms, and all around his head. The mother shoved her arm into the dog's mouth, and the mutt was happier to bite her. He tore chunks from her forearm and bicep and breast, then her thigh. She yelled for her husband who appeared at the back door with a handgun. He considered the angle so as not to hit his son or wife and blew the dog's head apart with a .44 magnum revolver.

The boy lay motionless in a small puddle of urine on the stretcher. I explained who I was and what I needed to do to help him, but he only stared at me. His face was small and round, his skin pale and mottled, his eyes hazel. I told him I had to cut his clothes away, asked permission to clean and bandage him, and he nodded but didn't stand. I rolled him on one side and then the other to remove the soiled pad and replaced it with a fresh one.

Now that the smell of urine was gone, I could detect the distinct odor of dog breath and dog food, the dry kibble kind. The punctures and tears looked like red polka dots across every visible area of his skin, except the legs. Both calves had flesh torn away, wounds about three fingers wide and bleeding. Frothy saliva from the dog's mouth still covered the larger wounds. The medics had wrapped the worst of them with pressure dressings. As I sheared away the boy's shorts and Spider-Man T-shirt, I heard his mother begin to sob beside us. The nurse was applying pressure dressings to her wounds—still bleeding heavily, bright red blood seeping out fast—but she only stared at her son and wept. I cried too, but the boy only gawked at me, beyond me, as I pressed bandages against his gashes, like plugging a hole in a Swiss-cheese-like dam, seeping out from everywhere at once but with only two hands and half a brain to stop it, and finally the boy's eyes streamed fat tears but without a grimace. He sat forward with a whimper like a wounded puppy and reached for my hand. I held pressure on a laceration with one hand and held him with the other. He looked at me now but not through me. I imagined the fierce snaps and tugs of the dog's jaw and teeth into soft flesh. The terror in the child's gaze punctured my eyes and deep into my brain and dropped into my heart above my churning gut. He let out a robotic "ouch," and my heart sank deeper, though I was in my own robotic mode, so he wouldn't match my emotions, wouldn't see just how terrifying this ought to be for him. Strict, sterile professional, always.

"We should do this more often, Dad," Dominik said. I could barely make out the sentence he was so far away, rummaging around the brush at the tree line for a stick. He picked up one, examined it for a moment, and tossed it back into the woods to search for another. I could hardly catch my breath, but I couldn't remember walking fast or up a hill. I looked into the woods to my right, the thick pines going dark and dense a hundred meters in. I looked left across the right-of-way field at the brush on the bank of the swampy river.

"Hey, slow down, Domo," I called. The sentence barely came out as I gasped, and I pushed a hand against my chest trying to rub the tension away before I got to him. He stopped looking for a stick and watched me approach. Once I caught up, he studied me for a second.

"Are you ready to go back?" I said.

He pointed to the woods. "Can we go this way and look for tracks on our way back?"

I said yes, and we made our way to a trail head covered in pine needles and flattened grass, faint ATV tracks here and there. Poachers frequented the area, hunting without permission and sometimes out of season, and probably came to the water by this trail or flushed deer out that way.

"Aw, there's mud in here, Dad. We can see the tracks easier," Dominik said.

"What do you see?" I said without looking down.

I scanned the woods, tried to assess where we were and estimate the distance to the road I knew ran parallel on the other side. The pines stretched high, and the cover above made it seem darker. The breeze wasn't strong enough to push through, and it felt like a vacuum. Quiet. Coiled. Dominik scurried ahead, and I lengthened my stride to keep up until I got winded several paces into the thick of the forest. I looked back to the trailhead, and it was a halo of light, far and faint now. Dominik picked up a stick here and there, eyed it, carried it for a bit or whacked a tree truck with it, and then tossed it back into the brush. The trail was only slightly worn from the poachers, and the grass reached my knees, Dominik's waist. We strolled side-by-side, and I felt my shoulders inching up tight, so I grabbed a stick of my own and swung it at a branch just above my head. Dominik grinned at this development.

The breeze wasn't strong enough to push through, and it felt like a vacuum. Quiet. Coiled.

"Oh, that's a good stick, Dad," he said, admiring the limb in my hand.

I smiled back at him as we came into a clearing, and I launched the stick as far and high as I could manage.

"What did you do that for?" Dominik said through a frown at the stick's path and then back at me.

"Didn't need it. It's just a stick. Besides, we have yours," I said, pretending to admire the slim branch in his hands. He carried it like a long, leafy rifle in both hands across his upper thighs, as if he'd been on a long patrol and the weight of it pulled his guard down.

A rustle in the brush by the trail just a few meters ahead sent a jolt through me to Dominik's shoulder, which I grabbed tight and pulled him behind me.

"What, Dad?" he said, too loud.

I shushed him and crouched enough to shift my line of sight to the brush.

I met his eyes and brought my finger to my lips, slow and deliberate, and quickly shifted my gaze back to the source of the sudden commotion. Listen and watch, I mouthed, knowing he'd search my face rather than the bush. I turned my head so my good ear faced the noise I'd heard, and I cut my eyes to keep watch. Nasal grunting and more rustling came from the shrubbery and thicket, and I relaxed—standing taller now—but still cautious, apprehensive.

"Just a hog, maybe a boar," I said through a breathy whisper by his head.

I wanted him to be cautious, but I wasn't as concerned. I searched the red clay in front of me and saw the marks, two round hoven shapes and a bilateral indentation much like a deer but shallower, less weight to press them down. I examined the trunks of the trees nearby and noticed a nearby patch of cleared wood, freshly rubbed bark just below it at the base.

Knowing a threatened boar might charge, I kept Dominik behind me and eased in a wide semi-circle path away from the shrubs. The sounds faded, but I cast a glance over my shoulder every four to five paces as we traipsed through the high grass, over pine needles, and stomped down briars, a few clinging stubbornly to my pants. I heard birds flitting and chirping through the treetops overhead as we reached a small path, which led to the edge of the woods. The clearing ahead stretched back to the edge of our neighborhood, fresh red clay and downed trees from the land development crew's previous week of work were the only obstacles between us and home. The birds shot out overhead and rose high.

"Look, Dad! Birds! They're so blue. What're they called?" Dominik said, pointing as they whirled and chirped around each other.

"Blue birds," I said.

Dominik stopped with a snort and looked back at me only halfway, his eyes cut to the side with a squint.

"Hey, don't look at me. I didn't pick it," I said.

We laughed as I caught up to him and wound our way back to the land of asphalt and sidewalks. Behind my smile, I wondered if there were any tracks leading away from the cleared land, if we'd have to find a park or a forest nearby to see more, if we'd have to go deeper into the forest and stay through the night to find more tracks, to keep up with the animals. I wiped beads of sweat from my forehead with my shirt and examined Dominik for a second. No sweat but he breathed with his mouth open and swung his arms wide trying to keep up. He saw me watching him.

"Dad, I'm tired. How far are we from home?" he said.

"Keep pushing, buddy. We're almost there." ■

WOODCHUCK

Late June clatter of sickle bars, then, if the farmer's
bones are true, three days while timothy's drying
in windrows, two more before the baling is done,
flatbeds roaming hobnailed fields while barns wait
empty, dust rising like prayers, the true stained glass
of those quickened years when that dark harbored
angels, emptied burlap the streets of paradise.

Stubble filled with slim snakes and threadbare mice
startled into light, exposed but let be, though before
a second crop greened and grew, came a slow search
for signs of woodchucks, burrows into which smoke
bombs were dropped, entrances sealed with dirt over
flattened feed sacks as we scanned for other exits
we could pour a deadly mix, bleach and ammonia.

Tonight I could conjure, deep beneath the loam, cozy
lives and families, invent signs and stories, intermingled
kingdoms, mammal and more, contemplate enlightened
ecologies, entertain folk predictions for lengthy winters,
but instead unearth one afternoon: my brother driving
the '43 Ford, a wealth of bales I'd stacked on back as
newer boys tossed them up, a jig-sawed balance of

capacity and stability which cut trips to the barn and yet
ensured that nothing fell, no snapped twine or spread hay
along the roadside, when into this pastoral stumbles,
stout and furred, a target for a truck-armed teen, and so
begins a frantic chase across the field, sharp twists and
unpredictable turns long minutes before the woodchuck
scambles to safety, and my brother dismounts to survey

whatever wreckage has ensued, stands astonished: God
damn, we didn't lose a single bale—hell of a job there,
while the whole crew clambers aboard so we can head
off to the barn, then on to baseball, just like in the movies,

all of us lean and tanned, immortal and god blessed
under elms and pines and blackbirds, over the sunlit
brook, our load of golden bales solid as bullion.

GEORGE PERREAULT

LABOR DAY

dry white stalks
bend stiffly into
the dregs of summer
as muted birds,
finches mostly—

some sparrows—
side-step toward
seed heads, reaping
the cone flowers, shasta
daisies, black-eyed

susans, rummaging
inside a lavender
till the whole bush
shakes its come-on
far and wide, and if

you'd sit with me a
few, the breeze
freshening now as
it slips down the
foothills—just a while—

we're given this day
and maybe the next,
hollow-boned birds
working the harvest—
come, catch your breath

GEORGE PERREAULT

BOOK REVIEWS

Cathryn Hankla. *Lost Places: On Losing and Finding Home*. Macon, Ga.: Mercer University Press, 2018. 288 pages. Softcover. $20.00.

Reviewed by Emily Masters

In her essay collection *Lost Places: On Losing and Finding Home*, Cathryn Hankla focuses on ways the concept of home manifests in various aspects of her life. Hankla is a poet, novelist, and has written a variety of essays including the ones gathered in *Lost Places*. Her previously published works include *Fortune Teller Miracle Fish* (2011), *Great Bear* (2016), and *Galaxies* (2017). In *Lost Places*, she takes readers on a journey to explore many of the places she has physically called home as well as the homes she finds in spiritual places and in other people. The collection includes previously published content, such as "Neighborhood of

Desire," "The Final Frontier," and "Natural Disasters," alongside fresh content for her readers including "God's Eyebrow," an essay examining Hankla's relationship to her mother; "Invisible Cities," a meditation on fighting fears far from home; and "The Indispensable Condition," which offers a place for Hankla to pause and question her beliefs.

Themes in Hankla's essay collection include homesickness, staying versus leaving, heartbreak, solitude, loss, love, family, and spirituality. She confronts stereotypes about Appalachia by portraying a complex region throughout her essays, revealing a diversity of experiences. She also paints herself in a complex light, sharing with readers both her triumphs and pitfalls in her search for home. Hankla's writing evokes a wide range of emotional response. Often, readers will find themselves laughing out loud but then will find themselves biting back tears. Hankla uses humor to address moments in her life when she feels like she is losing her sense of self, turning many moments of reflection into chances to connect to readers using laughter. The humor in the collection is balanced by Hankla's ability to turn a phrase, to express descriptions poetically, making scenes come to life on the page and creating emotions readers will feel as if they are their own.

In her essay, "Cleaning out the House," Hankla writes, "No substitute for the self, a house can still be a surrogate, experimental self, a personal cabinet of curiosities, an expression of one's tastes and travels, dreams, expectations—and neuroses." Throughout the collection, Hankla reveals herself through her definitions of home. Readers get a glimpse of who she is, of her failed relationships, of her triumphs, of her doubts and vulnerabilities, through a tour of her various homes, both ones in which she dwells like in "Dream House" and ones she returns to again and again like Hankla's writing community in "Scarlet Tanager."

In "Lost Places," the collection's title essay, Hankla characterizes Chaco Canyon in New Mexico as a place she travels for spiritual renewal and reconnection to herself. She is drawn to Chaco because of the mystery of the history, the hidden pieces she likes to imagine, just as she enjoys writing in these essays to uncover aspects of herself and those places which have affected her life. Like all the essays in the collection, the title essay is full of research and literary references Hankla uses to reinforce her themes of home and of self-examination.

One of the best essays in the collection, "My Life in Snakes," traces the ways in which snakes have slithered into Hankla's life at seemingly every turn, a constant in a world where at times, her definition of home is forever shifting. The snakes are haunting, yet familiar, primordial. The shift from fear to familiarity shows how adaptable humans are to make any place their home, although some homes might call out to us more than others. Hankla's writing throughout the essays will be relatable to readers who have ever felt out of place, homesick, or found a fluidity to their definitions of home.

While almost all of the essays in *Lost Places* fit in with themes of home, "Place as Language" sticks out like a sore thumb. It is more a meditation on novelist William Goyen's work than an examination on Hankla's relationship to home. In the essay, she takes on a far more academic tone than in the rest of the collection. As the essay placed right in the center of the collection, it serves less as a hinge and more as a broken joint between the essays at the beginning and the essays following "Place as Language." The essay is fine for a more academic analysis but feels out of place in a collection of such poetically written essays. Other than this essay, Hankla's collection is beautifully written, cohesive, and full of relatable moments and themes.

Julia Spicher Kasdorf and Steven Rubin. *Shale Play: Poems and Photographs from the Fracking Fields.* University Park, Pa.: Penn State University Press, 2018. 144 pages. Hardcover. $24.95.

Reviewed by Jessica Cory

In a recent interview with *Mother Jones,* renowned poet Julia Spicher Kasdorf shared that upon commencing *Shale Play: Poems and Photographs from the Fracking Fields* with award-winning documentary photographer Steven Rubin, she "was really determined to keep an open mind. My impulse was to defend rural people for whom making a living has become increasingly difficult. If fracking means you can keep your farm, am I going to stand in judgment about that? I didn't know."

Kasdorf's observant inquiry into hydraulic fracturing, known often as "fracking," provides an almost-unbiased assessment of the process and its effects on the communities she engages with (and is indeed herself a part of) in Appalachian Pennsylvania. In fact, the outcome of Kasdorf and Rubin's work considers not just the residents negatively impacted by fracking, but the impacts such an industry has on its itinerant workers, the environments it develops and leaves behind, and each one of us, whom are often implicated in its necessity.

Shale Play begins with a foreword by Barbara Hurd, who notes that "Kasdorf and Rubin remind us all that we all live, consciously or not, within the larger contexts of other people with other stories." This weaving of our own lives, whether we reside in a heavily-fracked area or not, with the lives of both the authors and their subjects, seems to be the meaning behind *Shale Play*. This book exists to show us the interconnections and few degrees of separation that link not only those in Appalachian Pennsylvania, but also the grandmother making tea on a gas stove in Oregon and the farmer struggling to make ends meet in North Carolina. While this book focuses on a particular region of Pennsylvania, it is truly representative of all of us.

Kasdorf and Rubin follow the foreword with a fairly extensive preface. They utilize several cited sources and are informed by highly credible works including *The Boom: How Fracking Ignited the American Energy Revolution and Changed the World* by Russell Gold and Tom Wilbur's *Under the Surface: Fracking, Fortunes, and the Fate of the Marcellus Shale*, among others. The preface may not be required reading for those quite familiar with the practice and its rise in southwestern Pennsylvania; however, for readers who reside outside of the area or are unfamiliar with the breadth and depth of fracking, the preface provides an excellent resource. It also gives additional information on Kasdorf and Rubin, particularly their connections to the region and their experiences surrounding fracking, which is quite helpful for readers who are new to their work.

This collaboration between Kasdorf and Rubin is multifaceted: part documentary, part history lesson, part raw beauty in the juxtaposition between what we think of as the "natural" world and the artifice resulting when humans alter these landscapes. Rubin captures fracking pads at dusk with shadowy oak leaves overhanging the frame, horses grazing mere feet from gas wells, and meetings between concerned citizens and elected officials in which the tension jumps off the page. In addition to Rubin's imagery, Kasdorf includes portions of a once-sealed record of a settlement reached between two Washington County residents and an energy conglomerate, notes from a zoning hearing board in Fayette County, and even a letter from "Mrs. Lois Bainbridge to Governor Duff" from the Pennsylvania State Archives.

Through her poems in this collection, Kasdorf invokes the language and personas of those whom she's met through her travels in the region. She is able to express their words and thoughts so articulately that it is, at times, difficult to remember that Kasdorf penned the poems, as it seems her subjects are speaking to the readers themselves.

The diversity of her chosen subjects also cements Kasdorf's claim to entering into this project with an open mind: she talks to a student whose family leased land for fracking hoping to pay for their children's college, only to come up $37,000 short; she talks to a man laying pipe, who wishes he "could make a living as a welder, / but for now, this is the best job I can get"; and to the "President of the Okome Conversation Club" as he "Returns from Reconstructive Surgery" following the removal of a tumor on his forehead, following years of exposure to "toxins [that] entered through sweat glands or tear ducts".

One of the wonderful and unique aspects of this collection is that, unlike some collections of photographs and poetry, the layout of the book allows readers to immediately envision the subjects addressed in the poems. For example, "On a Porch Across from the Shamrock Compressor Station, a Tiny Lady Tethered to an Oxygen Tank Chats with a Stranger" begins on the same page as an image of the Shamrock Compressor Station, complete with several homes in view directly across from it, allowing the reader to immediately have concrete imagery to help more fully appreciate what the poem describes. This correlation also occurs for the poem "What This Picture Can't Tell You," which begins opposite an image of three local residents leaning against a black Crown Victoria, "purchased for a bargain according to the man in the black shirt, / was built for cops, it's so fast," as the reader's eye wanders to a young, shirtless man and his tank-topped girlfriend as the former signs "the petition on the car trunk" and we learn that they "would not carry signs / across the bridge and back for cash".

Shale Play is an exceptional amalgam of imagery, poetry, politics, history, and humanity. Through its representations of gas and oil extraction occurring throughout southwestern Pennsylvania, we're shown the sacrifices made by people we'll likely never know outside of this book. We're also faced with the barren landscapes turned to slabs so that Kasdorf's speaker (who appears to be the poet herself) can "drive home and cook my groceries / on a gas stove", much like the rest of us who often give these "sacrifice zones" so little thought. ■

OLD DOGS

Over millennia, water and silica
seep into cells, until wood
becomes stone. So it seems as well
in all too brief a time, cell
by cell, old dogs turn
into sweetness, faces bleached
like ghosts, bones brittle and sharp
as fallen sticks, until all that remains
is the slow thump of love
and tail. Surely that weight
in our hearts is stone, the work
not of eras but days
and weeks, old dogs like quartz
in our petrified memory.

JANE SASSER

CHIAROSCURO

The shadow you cast is a darkness
in which we all flounder, wish
we knew more than the outline
of your life, black and white photos
we shuffle through, glimpses
that leave us to guess: you,
in a white shirt and cotton ducks
rolled up, crossing Rocky River
to church in the johnboat you called
the bateau. From the overhanging branches
at the shore, your paddle raised
in morning light, a snake sifts
from a tree, circles your arm,
sloughs to the water below.
Or you, home from the war,
crutches in hand, missing a step
on concrete stairs, how you spilled
through bright air, made the choice
to swing your mending legs to spare
your heavy head, how when you hit
and rolled, you felt them snap again.
Or you, driving a bus through the dark,
that time—so tired—you followed white line
up an exit and sat and wondered
how you'd come to this place, and how
you drove that bus down and back into night.

JANE SASSER

EVERY LEAVING

is a death,
even the ones I think
I desired, the packing
of wool sweaters

for morning walks
through falling leaves
to college classes,
or boxes numbered and taped

for the move from
a long-loved home,
or holiday guests
who crowded our rooms,

towels and plates piled
in the wake of flurried goodbyes,
whose absence now
is a haunting lack.

In January dark
so cold it could break
like actual ice
I will drop you

for your flight,
driving to work
and trying to think
of my students, who

will shuffle to class
in their wool sweaters,
dimly aware of their own
looming leavings, and you

will be somewhere overhead,
soaring through dawn,
back to the life
you have chosen as yours.

JANE SASSER

CONTRIBUTORS

Melissa Ballard studied fashion merchandising, worked retail, and was a bank teller and a public school camp counselor before attending college as a first-generation student. She has since worked as a speech-language pathologist and a college instructor. Melissa has written essays for *Belt Magazine, Brevity, Under the Sun,* and other publications.

David Black's work has appeared in *Now & Then, Zone 3, Tar River Poetry,* and *Appalachian Journal.* He is the former poetry editor of English Journal and has published four poetry collections: *Some Task, Long Forgotten and Other Poems* (2000, reprinted 2017), *The Clown in the Tent* (2010), *Shortcomings: Around the Grounds and Corner* (2017), and *Aspects of a Crosscut Saw* (2017).

Jonathan Burgess lives in upstate South Carolina with his wife, four children, and a Giant Schnauzer named Titus Andronicus. He has an MFA in Creative Writing from Converse College. He's the managing prose editor for *South 85,* and his writing has appeared in *The Remington Review, Catholic Exchange, O-Dark-Thirty,* and *Blood & Thunder.* His essay "Chai Party" was published in *War, Literature, & the Arts* and was also nominated for a Pushcart Prize.

Jessica Cory is a native of southeastern Ohio now residing in western North Carolina where she teaches in the English department at Western Carolina University. Her work has appeared in a variety of journals. She is also the editor of *Where the Sweet Waters Flow: Contemporary Appalachian Nature Writing,* forthcoming from West Virginia University Press.

Todd Davis is the author of five poetry collections and a limited edition chapbook. He edited the nonfiction collection, *Fast Break to Line Break: Poets on the Art of Basketball,* and co-edited the anthology *Making Poems.* His poems have won numerous prizes and have been published in *American Poetry Review, Iowa Review, North American Review, Missouri Review, Gettysburg Review,* and other journals, and he teaches at Pennsylvania State University's Altoona College.

Holly Day has taught writing classes at the Loft Literary Center in Minneapolis, Minnesota, since 2000. Her poetry has recently appeared in *Tampa Review, SLAB*, and *Gargoyle*; her books include *Walking Twin Cities, Music Theory for Dummies*, and *Ugly Girl*.

Davis Enloe is a graduate of Converse College's MFA program. His work has been published in *Barrow Street, Cold Mountain Review, Plainsongs, Chariton Review, Broad River Review, The Saint Ann's Review*, and most recently on *Hunger Mountain* online.

Caleb Gill was born in Louisville, Kentucky and attended Kent State University. He is currently living in Pittsburgh, Pennsylvania, earning his MFA from Chatham University.

Sandra Kolankiewicz's poems have appeared in *London Magazine, New World Writing, BlazeVox, Prairie Schooner, Bellingham Review, Gargoyle, Fifth Wednesday, ArGiLo, Per Contra*, and other outlets. Her chapbooks are available through Black Lawrence Press and Finishing Line Press. She teaches English in West Virginia.

Preston Martin has published poems in *New Ohio Review, Tar River Poetry, Iodine, Chaffin Journal, Kakalak, Snapdragon*, and other journals. He has poems in *Every River on Earth: writings from Appalachian Ohio* (Ohio University Press), *Heron Clan*, and in other anthologies. He lives in Chapel Hill, North Carolina.

Emily Masters is a senior English major at Berea College where she works as a teaching assistant for Silas House and as a student editor of *Appalachian Heritage*. She is from Monteagle, Tennessee, where she lives on a farm with her family. Her work has been published in *Still: The Journal* and *The Pikeville Review*.

Christopher McCurry teaches high school English. He is the cofounder of Workhorse, a publishing company and community for working writers.

Jennifer McGaha is the author of the memoir *Flat Broke with Two Goats*. Her work has also appeared in *Huffington Post, The New Pioneer, PANK, The Chronicle of Higher Education*, and other publications. McGaha earned her MA from Western Carolina

University and her MFA from Vermont College of Fine Arts. She currently teaches at UNC-Asheville.

Kathryn Milam is a graduate of the MFA in Writing and Literature program at Bennington College where she studied with writers Alice Mattison and Elizabeth Cox. She is the founder and artistic director of Readings on Roslyn, a literary salon held in her home that has hosted thirty-eight writers and more than 4000 readers. She lives in Winston-Salem, North Carolina, with her husband and two dogs.

George Perreault's poems have been nominated three times for the Pushcart Prize and selected for sixteen anthologies and dozens of journals. His recent work appears in *The American Journal of Poetry, Split Rock Review, Timberline Review,* and *South 85 Journal.*

Jane Sasser has published poems in the *The Sun, North American Review, Journal of the American Medical Association,* and others. She has two poetry chapbooks, *Recollecting the Snow* (March Street Press, 2008) and *Itinerant* (Finishing Line Press, 2009). She recently retired from teaching English at Oak Ridge High School.

Summar West's poems have been published in a variety of places, including *491, Appalachian Heritage, Appalachian Journal, Ellipsis, New South, Prairie Schooner, Still,* and *Tar River Poetry.* Born and raised in east Tennessee, she currently lives in coastal Connecticut with her partner and their two daughters.

Marianne Worthington is co-founder and poetry editor of *Still: The Journal.* She is author of the chapbook *Larger Bodies Than Mine,* winner of the 2007 Appalachian Book of the Year Award. Her work has appeared in *Grist, Shenandoah, Appalachian Heritage, 94 Creations, Pine Mountain Sand & Gravel, Kudzu,* and many other publications. She lives, writes, and teaches in southeastern Kentucky.

Amy Wright is the author of two poetry books, one collaboration, and five chapbooks. Her essays appear in *Brevity, Kenyon Review, Waveform: Anthology of Women Essayists,* and elsewhere. Most recently, her nonfiction was awarded a Writers at Work fellowship. She lives in Tennessee where she teaches writing, and co-edits *Zone 3* journal and Zone 3 press.